John Brown Smith

Resuscitated

A dream or vision of the existence after death. The soul before Satan and Lucifer, or the modernized Hades. Discourse of Lucifer on national, social, religious and scientific topics

John Brown Smith

Resuscitated

A dream or vision of the existence after death. The soul before Satan and Lucifer, or the modernized Hades. Discourse of Lucifer on national, social, religious and scientific topics

ISBN/EAN: 9783337309718

Printed in Europe, USA, Canada, Australia, Japan

Cover: Foto ©Lupo / pixelio.de

More available books at **www.hansebooks.com**

A DREAM OR VISION

OF THE

EXISTENCE AFTER DEATH. THE SOUL BEFORE SATAN AND LUCIFER, OR THE MODERNIZED HADES.

DISCOURSE OF LUCIFER ON NATIONAL, SOCIAL, RELIGIOUS AND SCIENTIFIC TOPICS, PRINCIPALLY ABOUT THE UNITED STATES OF AMERICA.

"WHAT IS WANTED AT PRESENT."

THE PSYCOGRAPH:

AN INSTRUMENT DESCRIBED, AND HOW TO COMMUNICATE WITH THE SPIRITS. THE FORCE IS ATTRIBUTED TO THE SOUL OR HUMAN BEING WHO MANIPULATES THE INSTRUMENT, AND NOT THE SPIRITS, AS IS GENERALLY BELIEVED.

THE INDUCTION-COIL AND ITS USES IN THE RESUSCITATION OF APPARENTLY DEAD PERSONS. HOW A DEAD MAN WAS BROUGHT BACK TO LIFE.

SACRAMENTO
LEWIS & JOHNSTON, PRINTERS, 410 J STREET,
1883.

PREFACE.

It was the intention of the author of this work to bring it before the public at a much earlier date—it being finished about October 1st, 1882—but owing to various causes, it was postponed from time to time. One of the principal reasons, however, was the moral courage required to bring such a work forward in an incomplete condition.

The writer is well aware of the deficiencies the reader may meet in the perusal of the book, and the reasons of this defect are pointed out on the last page.

In regard to Forestry, in which the writer is greatly interested, it has been proved since the work has been written that some reliance may be placed in the assertions made about the Sacramento Valley.

It has been ascertained that the late great inundations along the Rhine in Germany, as well as those along the Ohio in our own country, had their origin in the wholesale destruction of the forests, or the want of trees at distant elevations.

What happened there will, in the future, take place on a larger scale in the Sacramento Valley, if no hindrance is placed before the destroyers of forestry.

The ideas entertained as to what will occur about Lake Tahoe in the future, have had another proof, also, in one of those electric storms, when the waves are drawn skyward and then let fall suddenly, to dash against the shore and carry everything before them. As the trees gradually fall before the destroyers, so will these storms increase in number and greater force.

Several of the suggestions made in the book are now being carried out—one being the adoption of new devices to stop railroad trains, and the safer methods adopted in coupling the cars, and thereby lessening the loss of life. The railroad companies are also making an effort to bring suitable emigrants to people the foothills, all of which is of the greatest benefit to this State.

The visional part of the book—or rather, the part the Devil plays with Mankind—must be left entirely to the reasoning power of the reader. The ideas entertained about his diabolical highness have gradually changed, for it must be obvious to most persons that just in ratio as you make the so-called devil powerful, so must the greatness of the Deity be diminished Himself.

It is hoped the reader will kindly overlook the deficiencies met with in the book.

THE AUTHOR

Sacramento, California, May 19, 1883.

CONTENTS.

The Soul Leaving the Body	1
In Presence of St. Peter	3
In Presence of Satan	5
The Human Devils	9
The Office of the Devils	10
The Soul's Treatment on its Progression—The Methods Adopted	11
Treatment of Inebriates	16
Vice and Virtue Harnessed Together	18
Views About Labor	19
Hints to the Wealthy	20
Philosopher and Horse Jockey	22
Catholic, Protestant and Jew	23
Advancement	24
Psychology	26
Human Body Assuming New Form	27
American Politics	29
Female Suffrage	31
Danger to the Republic	32
Coming Nobility	34
Great Wealth to Benefit the Lower Classes	35
Strikes	37
Treatment of Inebriates	38
Effects of Treating	38
A Vision of Higher Spirits	41
Reasoning Power of Animals	49
Forestry	51
Destruction of Trees About Lake Tahoe	52
Useful Trees	55
School of Forestry	56
Hydraulic Mining	57
The Water Used for Irrigation	59
Security of Dams	61
Sacramento Valley—Its Future	61
The Nation's Debt and Taxes	63
Qualifications of Citizens and Candidates	64
The Jury System	65
Too Much Liberty to the Youth	65
Demoralizing Literature	67
Rational Recreation for the Young People	68
High Pretensions in Morality Tested	69

CONTENTS.

Arbitration in Private Life... 70
Reward to Wife Whippers... 71
Grand Weddings.. 72
Grand Funerals... 73
Adulterated Food and Quack Medicine............................... 74
Tests for Lead.. 75
Baking Powder... 76
Ladies' Beautifiers... 77
Medicine Adulteration.. 78
Arsenic to Fatten Cattle.. 78
Fraud Rejuvenators.. 79
Impure Ice... 80
Water Added to Lard... 81
Coffee Adulterants... 82
Sewage... 82
Laboring Class Safe Investment...................................... 83
Keeping Sunday.. 83
Opinion About Christianity.. 87
Public Land.. 89
More Security on Water and Land................................... 89
Railroads... 90
Government Railroads and Telegraphs............................... 91
Safe Building.. 92
Sanitary Matters... 92
Mob Law... 92
Sentimentality... 93
American Abroad.. 94
Public Schools... 96
Wanted... 97
Kindness to Animals... 97
Exercise.. 97
Ventilation... 98
Drainage... 98
Foreign Languages... 99
Naturalized Citizens... 99
General Intelligence..100
Supervision Over Printed Matter.....................................101
Suitable Voting Stations..103
Shall Women Work?..103
Psychic Force..107
Psychograph...109
Harness Nature..110
The Soul Discovered...111
Retaliation on Wife Whippers..112
Return, and Musical Birds...113
Life a Puzzle—Do Right...115
Man a Slave Still to His Passions....................................116
Rapid Descent...117
The Soul Returns to the Body.......................................117
Induction Coil—Its Uses...118
The Torture..119
Back to Life...121
The Deficiencies of the Work..122

RESUSCITATED.

I am pursuing a mercantile occupation in one of the towns of the Sacramento valley, California, and on the eve of the twenty-third of September, 1882, I retired early to bed, having been more than usually exercised in business, from early morning until the hour of closing. The usual hour to retire, for me, is about eleven P. M., sometimes later; but that evening, owing to great fatigue, or a similar feeling that overcame me, I retired at nine o'clock, and very soon thereafter an unusual drowsiness overcame me, and apparently I was asleep; and yet all about me in the room appeared to be in agitation, as if the furniture and bedroom were ascending. The feeling experienced was similar to ascending a mining shaft or a rapid moving elevator. This lasted but a brief space of time; the objects vanished, and I alone was rising upward without any apparent aid. It was like being drawn forward by some invisible but magnetic power, drawing me constantly towards a certain direction, as a magnet attracts particles of metallic iron.

The world left behind me, in spite of night and darkness, was transparent, so to say, before me, for I could see myself reclining on my bed in the room I then had occupied in my house, and to all outward appearances was sleeping soundly. I was thus able to view myself at an immense height, without any effort to make use of my optical sense. I was enabled to see in every direction equally as well, if I so desired, on my rapid rise upward, which had increased to much greater speed than at the beginning.

Then the world below began to grow smaller; other luminous bodies became larger and larger; stars became like moons; some of these moons assumed gigantic sizes on nearer approach, but these were left right and left below me, in the rapid flight upward which then had acquired a velocity difficult to describe. First a bright light appeared above me, in the direction towards which I was so persistently attracted, without the slightest aid of myself. This light, first only seen as a brilliant star, became brighter and brighter on approaching nearer, and finally shone forth or assumed the most brilliant colors of the rainbow, or the solar spectrum produced by the aid of a flint glass or bisulphide of carbon prism.

Then the light appeared to be divided and subdivided, emanating from millions of light-producing objects, through which was visible a central core or nucleus of white light, most brilliant to behold. Shortly after, I could make out that the millions of minor lights issued by reflection or refraction by a greater light from millions of windows of a gigantic building or palace. Then I recognized human looking beings rushing upward on the same principle and speed as myself, all going in one direction, as if attracted towards the light or palace above. Finally, I came near the brightest light, situated far above on a tower, too high ever to be seen on the world below called earth. This tower, with noble and artistic architecture, of which men in our world have no conception, was built above one of the gateways, through which a constant stream of human looking beings poured into a large court. The magnificence of the whole surroundings were such that it would be difficult to describe, nothing being equal in beauty in the world man inhabits.

I mentioned human looking beings pouring through the gates. They seemed to be of human aspect, and yet some great change must have taken place; they appeared like shadows, almost transparent, doing things without any effort, as if muscles, bones and sinews were not necessary. The palace into which we entered was of such size that many Londons could be hidden in it, and its beauty was so magnificent that the revelations of St. John, "seeing New Jerusalem," were but a faint description of beauty when compared with the greatness and beauty of this building. This only refers to the exterior part, or what was then visible of the inner parts. No conception can be had probably, unless permission is earned to view it by those entitled to be there. From the court a stream of souls, from all nationalities and colors, representatives of the five races— or from the purest blonde Caucasian, to the darkest type of the African negro of both sexes—poured into an inner room, or large hall, and from there, in groups of twelve, they entered another room, through a small door. Before this door there were stationed two guardians in most elegant livery, one on either side of the entrance. They were of pure Caucasian blood, with long, yellow hair falling upon their shoulders. They possessed the anatomy of men, and yet, in their youthfulness, seemed more related to the opposite sex than the stronger. Although like human beings, there was still something more elevating or noble about them, than the crowd they were surrounded with. Another of the same species arranged and regulated the groups as they marched through the small door of the inner room. Only when brought in closer proximity did those human-like beings show their greater size, and more perfect stature and physiognomy.

In spite of the rapid and business-like management to pass group after group through the door by the attending officer, it took quite a time before my time came to enter the next room. In being marched through the door, I was the last of the twelve to enter.

Only two persons, or officers, were present, besides the new comers, after the usher had left. One was a tall, white haired and whiskered old gentleman, talking like a commander, and apparently the principal; the other was a much younger man, and represented the subordinate. Both held long scrolls of parchment in their hands, which they compared, as one by one was passed through a door. The names were given when asked, and then the scrolls of parchment were consulted, and being found correct, the being was transferred beyond the door by the attendant. When my turn came, as the twelfth and last, the old gentleman asked, "Your name, sir?" to which I answered, Jones Brown Smith. The old man looked up in astonishment, repeating the names, and adding, "that's a powerful combination you carry for your name; it must be a perfect safeguard at the post office window to secure all your letters without being previously opened by another member of the great Smith family. We find the representatives of the Browns, Jones, and Smiths, very strong here, coming from England and the countries they originally settled, but never have I found them thus united before. It is right clever—right clever, indeed," he repeated, and then searched the records of the scroll in use, and after some time, requested his attendant, also, to look over his own, but there was something wrong apparently. After repeated searchings, he said: "It is very strange, but your name cannot be found on the list of those called in, so there must be some unaccountable mistake beyond my comprehension. You see, here they come first when they arrive, and pass through those two doors, to the right and left, after my examination. All who preceded you of the group you entered with, have gone through the larger door to the left. You will notice the right hand door is very small, and through that not one in ten millions is found in proper celestial condition to enter; nearly all have to pass to the other side of this extensive palace, where they will be taken in charge by the chief of that establishment and his numerous assistants, as refractory and rebellious material, to be hammered and worked into proper shape and form, intellectually taken, you know."

"This Chief is known below as one who goeth about like the British lion—beg pardon, I meant a roaring lion—seeking whom he may devour. Up here he bears a better name, and is like all of us, but a servant to the Higher Power, who has willed to bring your kind to a higher state of perfection under our supervision, since so very few below are of their own accord in a proper condition to be admitted through that little door there. This Chief, therefore, acts in the capacity of a warden, or the head of a vast reformatory; and I assure you he understands the office intrusted to him exceedingly well, unlike your officers below, who often have but little capacity or knowledge of the office they occupy, but leave it in the hands of the subordinates almost entirely.

"As your case is not clear to me, I cannot pass you through the door your predecessors went; my advice is, therefore, to retrace your steps out of this part of the palace by the way you entered. When outside, pass along the continuation to the left, or bounding north. That part is not illuminated as it is on this side; nevertheless, the great illumination on the southern part aids to light it up sufficiently for all purposes. No extra lights are visible except at distant intervals, but these lights are not of the brilliancy they possess here. Well, Mr. Smith, when you arrive at the first entrance outside, over which you notice one of those lights, you enter, and having passed the portal you soon will be met by an official who will conduct you direct to the governor of the establishment, who is gifted with the knowledge why you are before us. In the meantime au revôir, Mr. Jones Brown Smith, and should you come again I will assuredly be in a mental condition to understand how to proceed with you."

He bowed and shook hands, and so did his attendant, and I passed out. Some delay must have occurred during my examination, for on being out I noticed several groups drawn up, and some waiting impatiently to be directed to their proper places. Some astonishment was naturally manifested on perceiving me, an ordinary being just arrived from below, leaving the intended new abode; but I passed out, and took the direction requested to take. The part directed to was found to be a continuation or extension of the place, a sort of division from the brighter part. The architecture, judging from the exterior, was less artistic and noble than the other part. Yet, when comparing it with edifices below, it far surpassed them in beauty of design. The light shed over it at the time was sufficient to notice everything of note quite well. This part of the structure extended for miles and miles, north, and appeared the largest part of the building. It seemed sufficiently large to hold ten times the population of the earth, for it must be remembered that I passed along in front at a rate of speed quite different from a human being. I had traversed at least forty or fifty miles in front of the building in a short space of time. There was no physical effort in my progression—it only required my will-power to propel me along. The attraction, however, I formerly experienced had ceased. I went along quite independent of it, and by my own acquired or mental effort.

The progression could not be compared to flying or walking, or any locomotion by which earth's creatures propel themselves forward. It was more on the principle of a balloon traversing the air, excepting that with me it required only a foot or less elevation from the ground, as I rapidly went forward, until I came to the first entrance, which was sparingly illuminated from above. A tower was built over the entrance, but the light did not shine forth from a high elevation, nor was the tower pretentious in appearance; it rather could make claims to solidity and great strength, being built short and massive, corresponding however with the size of the building upon which it was reared. I passed the gate and had proceeded but a few steps when I was met by a tall, well formed gentleman, just of the age when manhood has acquired its greatest physical strength. This man was plainly but neatly attired, and his person impressed one at once that the duty assigned to him would be carried out to the letter, after it was intrusted to him.

His eyes rested on me, and they seemed to search every nook and corner of the soul of my soul before him. Such eyes had never looked upon me previously, excepting the yellow haired guards and attendants of the first station visited, who had similar organs of sight, but less searching and penetrating than the one before me then.

For form's sake he inquired my wants; but, as I could give no definite account of myself, he answered:

"I have read your thoughts, know your wants and the reason why you visit here; but, as the matter is beyond my control, my duty compels me to bring you before our Principal, who alone is authorized to pass judgment in your case, for he rules here, but only under the guidance and will of a still Higher Power, to whom all must bow and submit. We are all here but as servants to carry out the will that is destined to be. In the end all will be well."

He then preceded me, and we passed through numerous labyrinths of corridors, passages, and halls, until we finally arrived at the door of a room which unceremoniously opened itself to admit us. The room was spacious and well provided for business purposes. At the extreme end there was a somewhat elevated space, with railing about it, which seemed designed to be the place for the chief or principal of the room. There were neat shelves filled with books of all imaginable languages, some ancient scrolls of parchment upon which I espied hieroglyphics probably dating back many thousand years. Everything denoted a modern spirit in the upholstery, convenience and comfort of an office occupied by an intelligent and progressive individual. Several devices in use were not even known to me yet, and the light that came from above, too, was such that it shed a mellow, soft radiance equally all over the room, without having any tendency to affect the sight or cause any pain, should such beings as were before me ever be afflicted with pain. In the middle of the inner office sat a gentleman of about the same age as the one who conducted me. He was, however, taller and of magnificent form, and to us below he would look as a giant in stature, but as all his attendants and assistants present in the room were about of the same age, the same noble figures and bearing, the size would not be impressed upon one's mind. Only when I looked upon my own deficiency was I made acquainted that these beings were of superior size and nobler creation than man below. The conductor brought me forward and bowed, which was gracefully returned to both, and then left without giving any cause why I was brought before him. As he left the room the door noiselessly shut itself again, and on suddenly turning I found two penetrating eyes surveying me from head to foot. The same feeling overcame me as before, but more severe. My intellect, memory, and feeling were disturbed to such an extent as if these mental qualities had simultaneously been tumbled down, as the ball knocks down the ten-pins in the play, and as the pins were reset, one by one, so my reason returned to its proper cells or station.

The gentleman then addressed me thus: "Mr. Jones Brown Smith, I have searched the inner recesses of your soul, and have learned the past and all former connections you had with the world below. For some reason, which would be incomprehensible to you if informed at present, you have arrived before your time. The soul of the body below which you have occupied has not yet been summoned, therefore the old gentleman on the other side has not found you on his list. Although he occupies a most responsible position, and has acquired great tact by his constant attendance to the departed souls from below, coming from all nationalities, he is yet like one of them, being born of woman. He has not the faculty to read, at once, the being before him—read the good deeds and the bad ones committed during a lifetime. It was not designed thus; his office only extends to admission, and he has the faculty to select the one he may find in about ten millions of souls brought before him who may have proved to have led a better life. It is very easy to distinguish such souls—he could not overlook them—and the guardians, also, are of a higher class, who would give information if the knowledge had not been acquired. When the clock has run down below that the Almighty has wound up, when the world has come to an end, when the harvesting is done, and all souls gathered in, then Peter's office ceases, and then an opportunity is given for him to advance to our comprehension.

"You think, I perceive, that such an office ought to be rewarded with advancement at once, but this cannot be tolerated any more than a university of great repute would grant a diploma to an ignoramus. The cook and porter of the university may have honestly served a quarter of a century, but that never made them students entitled to the honors of a diploma. All here must earn the intellectual advancement before any rise higher in station can take place. Such toleration would wreck the whole heavenly laws, began ages before your little planet had any signs of life upon it.

"It was mentioned to you that your soul has not been summoned yet, which signifies that it must return to its housing, outer shell, or body, and there reside and act until the time arrives when the proper agent is instructed to do his duty—the agent is Death. But being here, I will grant you the liberty which very few mortals have enjoyed thus far, that is, being shown over this great reformatory. It is not alone, I must admit to you, to gratify you, but also to change the contemptible views humanity has entertained, and is entertaining of us still, thereby not only lowering us, but lowering the qualities of the Most High. By this time, without further introduction, you have probably learned that I am he who is called Satan below, of whom you have often seen, heard and read—flattering his anatomy and qualities, ironically speaking. Take courage, and look upon me well; also, take in a full view of all my assistants in office here. Are we as represented below? Are we not, without flattering ourselves, even superior to your species below? And why not, since we are created to be your schoolmasters and teachers, bringing your souls to a proper elevation for advancement, or giving the rudimentary teachings to advancement on the other side by wiping out, erasing, and neutralizing the grosser passions which have been fastened upon your soul during a lifetime. Only one in about ten millions is ever passed direct through the little door where the old gentleman presides. You can judge from this that the labor to be carried out must be gigantic, having seen the great number who are admitted continually; and sometimes, when great battles are fought; epidemics visit the earth; an earthquake takes place; fire, water, wind, and electricity is turned loose, to cause destruction, then old St. Peter is very busily engaged; and we are no less here, to place them in their proper positions, which will be explained to you subsequently.

"The terrible pictures imparted to you of us by paintings and stories are a myth, and a gross libel upon us. Tails, cloven feet, horns, cross-eyed vision, a deformed body; all these have been pasted and labeled upon us, and the first time we appeared we were even a despised snake, for which few animals entertain any love or attachment, much less reasoning man. Spiritually, the Darwinian theory would have shown itself energetically when a snake is transformed in the space of five or six thousand years to beings of our class, but the Great Power that brought us into existence also wrought you, and it is in your likeness.

"The Devil or Satan has ever been termed a liar, and yet there is no greater liar than man himself. Your priesthood, from the beginning of the world's history, amongst many creeds and nationalities, have all told their lies, impressed their fears, and charged us in the end with everything which the viciousness of your kind has brought upon itself. From the beginning of your Jewish, Christian and Mahommedan religion, the Devil is charged with the sins of the world, by teaching disobedience, in the shape of an ugly reptile. Eve blamed the Devil, and Adam was manly enough, as his name implies, to blame his wife. Much of this sort has been continued since the world's history. Every ailment, ill luck, punishment by natural laws or the written laws of man, is laid at the door of the Devil, if no other tempter is found.

"The Devil and the lie is born with you, and frequently manifests its signs at an early age, without the aid of the so-called devils. The little girl and boy, at an early age, learns to lie, and in order to escape threatened punishment, will throw all blame of little sins or indiscretions committed, upon one of the family, if the discovery is made. Then we are made the instigators who put these ideas into the head or charged the reasoning power of the child, woman or man to commit acts which your laws forbid and which only too often all have carried out. Think you we have not more important work before us to put in proper condition the gross souls we receive from below? Would there be a grain of wisdom displayed if, by vile temptations, we increase crimes, make you more vicious and refractory, brutalize you to the lowest animals, and then, it being our duty to pull you out of the mire of misery and elevate your soul to a higher social standard? No, my friend Smith, our ambition is not to increase our labor as an experiment—we know your species quite well here and the world below. We know, only too well, the good and bad rests with yourself. A great deal is inherited and much is acquired in vicious company. The animals show it also quite frequently. Why is one horse more gentle, more obedient, less wild, often showing more intelligence, less stubornness and more confidence? Much lies in the breed and inheritance from the parents, the greater part in the early training, which under judicious management, force and gentleness, applied just in proper time, will break the wildest colt and make him obedient to man.

"This principle you can apply to other animals and to your children. A passion, destructive to the child, nourished by the parents, will destroy that child, when a young woman or young man. The fault must be pulled out by the root by force and gentleness properly applied. The Deity makes the parents responsible for the crookedness of the child. When young, the uneven place, morally speaking, ought to have been straightened out by gentle pressure, by main force if necessary. When older, the method has become impossible—the crooked place, fault or crime has been growing with body and soul and cannot be rectified. Often the negligence has to be partially atoned in your world already by parents and children both.

"One of your wise men, in an old book set up to guide you, has written: 'Spare the rod and you spoil the child.' There is much truth in it, yet the rod, for the young human being and the animal, has often caused the reverse. A proud and sensitive horse does not require the lash; a firm, steady hand and kind words and treatment may often accomplish more. Neither do sensitive children require constant and cruel corporeal punishment, for it breaks their spirit, makes them indifferent, and instead of making good men makes them revengeful. There is a time for everything, and the young must be attended to before it is too late, but judiciously.

"These are ideas we entertain here in spite of being charged of going about like a roaring lion seeking whom we may devour, or of throwing temptations to humanity as a bait to lead them astray.

"Who would trust or be tempted by a poor and ignorant looking Devil, who makes his appearance in such ugly shapes, in such rude and frightful ways as you have them coming amongst you—fine and tempting figures to win your fastidious human beings to commit wrong against each other. If the Devil was to appear in the shape of a beautiful female, there might be some chance to make your young as well as gray-headed and bald-headed men sin, against their will of course, but in the shape he generally is said to make his appearance, he would have but little success. Your human devils are better experts to bag their game. If ever we need any more work, we can find an abundance of material amongst you to answer our purpose. The reason we do not has been given already.

THE HUMAN DEVILS.

"The real devils of your world are not of that class—they are not like roaring lions, not rough prize fighters, highway robbers or rough looking convicts. These men are spotted as your police terms it. Many are against them—they are too open, too candid, show their cards on first acquaintance, and no one courts their company or has any faith in them.

"Your real human devil is a sleek fellow in broadcloth, who with devotion's visage and pious actions sugars over the devil so that he himself appears as a saint. He belongs to some fashionable church where the usher nor the congregation would be pleased to seat Jesus Christ, were he to pay a visit of inspection, unless he were dressed in fashionable broadcloth. He performs all sorts of charitable acts that cost little and where he is sure the world will hear of it. He belongs to numerous benevolent societies; he has the confidence of the widows and orphans; he manipulates money for others in order to bear a good percentage, for he is supposed not only to bear the virtues of honesty and to be a good christian, but also to carry out great business enterprises for the sake of others whose money was entrusted to him. Some fine morning he does not appear at his place of business—somebody's daughter in high life is also missing; later in the day the bank or business place finds money and securities gone; the same day the wife and six children also miss their pious father; the creditors, widows, orphans, and working people miss their money and benefactor (?).

"These are some of the human devils who throw out more deceptive inducement to do injury than we can; and these human devils, when placed under our care, often cause us unusual anxiety to put them on the path of progression. But there are so many devils below, and mankind is so depraved and wicked, it requires no outside pressure to cause them to be worse. The Devil resides with every human being, and if you allow him to control you, he will take possession of you. THE PASSIONS ARE YOUR DEVIL.

"But my time is limited, Mr. Smith. I am compelled to pass you over to Mr. Lucifer, one of my assistants of the inner department—a very energetic and intelligent member of this reformatory. He will show you over a portion of this extensive establishment, give you information, possibly instruction, and guide you, for what semi-mortal being could ever find his way out again from the passages of this great palace?"

As if summoned, a somewhat younger appearing gentleman entered from another apartment, and bowing politely to both, cast his eyes upon me, when the same strange, peculiar feeling overcame me, as already stated. The eyes expressed to me what words would, and the language was, "I know you, and your life's history, as I have known millions before you who have entered here."

Then Satan requested Lucifer to guide me, and show the various methods adopted to bring the rebellious spirits into subjection, or, like rough diamonds, grind them down, to show their true value.

THE OFFICE OF THE DEVILS.

We both bowed ourselves out, I rather following the politeness of my guide than my own will, and having closed the door, Lucifer stopped, remarking, "You need not be alarmed Mr. Brown Jones Smith, for you will not be compelled to see, or witness anything that will shock your feelings. The high pressure Hell your priests preach about, does not exist, and if it did, would be of no consequence, for if you reason as an intelligent being, as I take you to be, the influence that can be brought to bear upon a body like a human being, of flesh and blood, would have not the slightest effect upon the soul. A thing lighter than vapor, a being without substance, cannot be tortured by methods your holy inquisitions adopted to force people to believe certain lies against their will, or cause them to divulge great secrets. No; these foolish stories have been trumpeted about long enough to frighten the ignorant and children. The intelligent never invested in the foolish stories, although many preached them, and preach the old, trumped-up lies still, to keep, or try to keep, the ignorant in subjection. Then why should it be necessary for us to assume the horrible shapes you have given us below? Why take delight in torturing you, and be greater criminals than yourself? Do you select the outcasts, and most abandoned and criminal men, to superintend your reformatories, penitentiaries, work-houses, and similar institutions you have below? Do you not generally pnt in such offices tolerably good men, with a fair reputation, in order to be respected, not only by the general public, but the criminals themselves must have faith in them, knowing them to do justice to them and the offices they occupy. Why, then, should He, who rules over all, select such miserable beings as we have been, and are yet represented below, to torture your immortal souls forever and ever? We are here to carry out His will and wisdom. We are the wardens, the governors, the superintendents, the teachers and instructors, and do but our duty under a higher government, precisely as man does below. The salary is about the same as the priest receives that wanders among a dangerous tribe of Indians, endeavoring to Christianize them, or like the Sister of Mercy, and similar noble societies of other religions, or no religion at all, if you will have it, who venture on the battle-field when bullets and bombs fly about to do their deadly work, to attend to the wants of the wounded and dying. To the same classes I may add some of your noble physicians—of all civilized countries, or those who go amongst your cholera, black pest, and small-pox patients, or who, in contagious diseases of that nature, render assistance without fearing to sacrifice their own lives.

"This only is our reward, to do good to the soul as those try to do good to the body—sometimes soul, too. What matters it to you, when in your death struggle your parched lips receive the cup of water held in the hands of a woman who professes a different religion? Is it less sweet? These are truly acts of christianity, be they carried out by Catholic, Protestant, Jew, or the non-believer. You all stand on equal footing here, all have to be intellectually trained and worked in order to advance you. There is punishment, as you will perceive, but it mus affect the soul and have a tendency to improve it morally, causing it by its own will-power to rise higher and higher.

THE SOUL'S TREATMENT ON ITS PROGRESSION—THE METHODS ADOPTED.

"I will now briefly explain to you the beginning or treatment of new arrivals. You see this vast corridor, extending miles and miles into the interior. There are thousands of these extending in different directions. You notice there are doors on each side, certain distances apart. Behind these doors are small rooms or cells, occupied by two new arrivals. To make the matter clearer, the members of the group you entered with all passed through a certain door, leading into a corridor or passage that connects this part of the structure with the other. The shades of the departed are received separately by the proper attendants, who at once, by their spiritual gift or sense, examine the soul and its past life when occupying its human garment, shell, or housing, or when in flesh and blood. The whole history and its ruling passions are at once revealed to them that occurred in its lifetime; from this, as any professional man would do, the method adopted or to be pursued is chosen. The physician, knowing the disease, must find the proper remedies, and so do we, and I am sorry to state like the man of medicine we often are not quite successful first in adopting the usual remedies. In nature, it is said, the Creator made nothing alike. It is true, the similarity is very great to the eye, so that one might swear that a leaf is precisely like the other one; or that egg, that fruit, of the same size and color; but your men of science, who manipulate delicate balances, find differences in weight. By the aid of their instruments they arm your eyesight so it can see a thousand fold better. Now examine your leaves again and see the great changes in their structure. The same difference would be exhibited if the minutest animalcule could be accurately examined. The same you may apply to physical and mental parts of man, and the soul itself has its qualities. There is the temperament, the habits acquired, the vices which have fastened themselves like parasites upon the soul when in the body and could not be dislodged as long as life lasted. This, and much more, is to be considered before the improvements begin. But we know the grossest or predominating vices of the soul at once, and against these we operate first, before we begin on the minor sins.

"Now, returning to the duties intrusted to us and comparing your teachings below of nearly all religious denominations, it must be admitted that we devils play a far more important, or rather powerful part, than we are entitled to; but all the power attributed to us is taken away from the Almighty. There is certainly something contradictory in the teachings which makes God allwise and almighty, signifying to know the distant future and to exercise the greatest power in the universe, and yet allow the miserable devil to eliminate all his good work which he designed for man. After making all creative things to his satisfaction, he permits a subordinate spirit to undo all his work again, requiring a change in the programme.

"One of your holy books mentions, that if the first created human beings had not disobeyed the Deity, everything on your little world below would have been heaven-like already. We make no investment from our capital of knowledge in that doctrine, for it would signify that you were to lead a life of idleness and inactivity. If it was designed that life was to be sustained by eating and drinking, wearing garments and to live above the brute creation, it was also designed that you should be your own provider, your own builder, your own protector, for without cultivating your mental power or your mind, without profiting what you gradually learned by dearly purchased experience, you would never have attained the higher state of civilization. The natural wants for food, the requisite artificial covering for your bodies, when in a lower state of civilization, gave constant employment to the mind, which gradually brought you to a higher state and gave you means to live more refined. You are the only creative beings who have elevated themselves to the present state of civilization, but it was designed to be by your own energy, by your industry and experience. Abundance does not produce the highest intellect, nor is it positive that the greatest wealth must be centered in a country where nature is prolific in her gifts. Often the natives of such lands belong to a lower scale of civilization than those living in a less favored climate, because the mind is never sufficiently exercised or compelled to be, nature furnishing all immediate wants in close proximity.

"The Great Spirit designed, during the geological ages while the earth was being prepared, that you should be the rulers and the world be populated by your kind, and he meant also that you should be your own providers; therefore, your ancient nations found it already to their advantage to cultivate the soil artificially, and not rely upon wild game or fruit wherever it is found or caught by the savage, and to this great resource, agriculture, as the population increases, it is more and more necessary to pay attention. But all signifies labor. If the first theory was to be admitted, the ground would yet be untilled, thousands of discoveries and inventions would not be even thought of, or could be comprehended, for in order that anything be understood it must be of some benefit to body or mind. The hog cannot appreciate a looking glass, but the most ignorant savage may find delight in viewing his reflection. It is, however, no absolute want, for the savage can do without it. To the civilized man these auxiliaries are of more importance; they can really become wants.

"There are thousands of human beings who would be willing to eat less every day, than to forego the reading of the daily newspaper, which has become intellectual food to them, gratifying their desires to know what great events have taken place during a short space of time in your world. The untutored would take the grosser material or would rather fill his stomach.

"One of the prime factors in the advancement of the human race to its present elevation was necessity. It will continue to play an important part in the constant change which your globe is compelled to undergo. The ever busy and creative mind of man also has done much, and at this age, reward, which means acquired wealth— money—money is the powerful lever by which they try to gain their end and happiness while their lives last.

"In the end, money is but the servant; but intellect, the mind of man, is the designer, the creator; frequently the designer, the creator, the originator of great enterprises, as the discoverer, inventor, and composer is, however, in such a condition as to be compelled to lead a miserable life, while the one who supplies the money, reaps all the benefits and honors. As civilization rises still higher, the services of such men and women must receive better compensation.

"Great things have been accomplished, but greater yet will the never resting spirit of man carry out in the future. The Creator gave you the material in a rough state; out of it the sculptor chisels the statues of the gods; the mechanician builds those gigantic engines where, by the confining of two great forces, you are swiftly carried over land and sea, and often creates a force of thousands of human beings. A little child, after necessary preparations, may cause a city to be destroyed or lift the mountain top from its main foundation, in order to lay bare the much coveted yellow metal which your nation worships as a deity. All this the mind accomplished and labor carried out, and had the Ruler designed that you should live in idle luxury, you would have been deficient in intelligence, for want of mental and physical exercise."

"But, Mr. Lucifer, if God willed so, it could be carried out, for it is in His power to produce miracles," I suggested, or took courage to say.

He smiled peculiarly, and answered: "Yes, according to your

teachings below, he produced many miracles—some in which vainglorious man might delight were they really true. According to your early belief, which is yet a sort of corner-stone or foundation of several, or a number of religious denominations, the so-called universe was specially designed, because amongst it a little planet, or star, known as Earth, revolves, and the whole was particularly created, because upon this planet there lives a superior animal known as man. Reflect, Mr. Smith, upon the millions of fixed stars and planets created alone for your gratification. A grain of sand created wants to be gratified by having countless grains of sand on the shore of a vast ocean as companions. The Great Power created the gigantic elephant in order to gratify its parasite. It is extreme vanity or ignorance which can believe such assertions at the present age. The laws of nature are fixed; there is a mutual attraction and a mutual benefit; one is but a link; it requires a number to make a chain; together they form a whole. A wheel taken out of your clock causes derangement, or the stopping of the time-piece, as one wheel is necessary for the others; all have their special duty assigned by the man-creator, and should God act less wise than his creature?

"Further on, a good man makes the sun stand still, or what is by your present laws of astronomy equivalent to stopping the earth. Have you reflected what the consequences would be if a solid body the size of the earth, flying in its orbit with inconceivable velocity, or over nineteen miles per second through space, were suddenly stopped? Would it be reasonable to credit that the Deity would submit to having a world destroyed to gratify a man who has undertaken to annihilate a whole nation? One medicine man of an inferior Indian tribe works upon the superstitious intelligence of his people, and prays to God that the sun stand still, in order to be enabled to carry out the cruel work of murdering and destroying a superior tribe and possess their land. Where is the proof that God instigated the idea, that this diabolical deed was carried out? The blame is not deposited at our door, for we poor devils had but little to say, and do yet, in those days, as far as your book goes. Farther on we are supposed to have made our appearance again. Leaving the past ages, we will pay attention to the present, and what you are to see and be instructed in.

"Now I will raise the wicket of the third cell on the right, into which please take a look. Yes, you are right, two men—two souls, better expressed—and I will add, who have but lately arrived, being but a short time before your arrival in the main office. Their history, briefly told, is this: they are, like you, Americans; one died a drunkard, the other a straight-laced temperance man. A TEMPERATE man may imply much more. Generally, in your country, a temperance man is a man who abstains from indulging or partaking of any kind of beverage charged with alcohol. But for all this, such a man may nevertheless be very INTEMPERATE in eating, in the use of tobacco, or wherever a man can be intemperate. There are many reasons why a person may be termed intemperate, although he may be a perfect fanatic upon the use of alcoholic beverages. The one to the left was such a man, and withal an extreme fanatic, hating and condemning all he came in contact with who used any kind of liquors containing alcohol. He was extremely narrow-minded and irrational in his views, and yet he was not a criminal, or committed any gross sins of note. The one to the right was a slave to king alcohol, which robbed him of all—wealth, station, office, wife, children, relatives and friends. At one time he held a position in your nation, standing high in his profession, but by his passion all was sacrificed. He fell lower than the swine, for they would not keep company with him in the gutter; and yet this man hardly ever wronged a man, had a noble disposition, and when able, did much good in a quiet way. Those he befriended stepped over his prostrate body; they were the first who turned their backs upon him and disowned him. Why did he learn to drink? You know the causes are many; sometimes it is the love the person entertains for it from childhood up. It is born with the human being—a sort of inheritance, which is difficult to resist. It was not the case with this man, who was excellently brought up, had a good and loving mother, and a straightforward, honest father. The people were in easy circumstances, and he received an education which enabled him to advance readily in a first-class college. He was married to one of the belles of New York, a society lady, who was in the habit of being attracted to all fashionable meetings. The woman was coquettish, but true to her husband; but a reputation assailed by some enemy, and that enemy a woman who was envious of the attention paid her, caused the husband to lose faith. The green-eyed monster was aroused in him, and suspicion and coincidence did the rest, and he took refuge in the cup, becoming an outcast. She found a refuge with her parents, and about a year ago died a sorrowful woman. The woman was much to blame at first, for she had neglected husband and children both, and yet she meant no wrong, like thousands of other married women before her.

"Here, then, we have the opposite; here is their hell. See how the temperance man glares upon the drunkard, and how cowed down the other is, knowing his great infirmity. How quick these two would leave each other and find more suitable company if they could only pass out of the cell. Do you know it is suffering a mental hell to have a human being constantly with you whom you dislike and despise? Have you ever been on board of a ship, and cooped up in a small cabin with a disagreeable companion who is the very opposite to you? If you ever have, you have a faint idea of torture in a spiritual sense on earth. Here it is greater, for they have the faculty of interchanging thoughts rapidly, without the aid of speech, if they choose; but they gradually have the rough corners worn off as they subdue their human vices and gross passions. It is very difficult with some at first to make any progress. The old Adam, or man of earth, is so closely bound up with the released soul, yet, or the latter finds itself estranged it cannot act independently. But I assure you they all advance in course of time, and some quite rapidly, after the feeling from below, not in sympathy with the place here, is suppressed. The drunkard here is the better man, more open, and entertaining no malice and petty spites, like the narrow-minded shade of the other man. He acknowledged his infirmity, but could not control the powerful passion that governed his whole body while in life.

TREATMENT OF INEBRIATES.

"It were far better if those addicted to strong drink, whether rich or poor, were treated similar to the insane; that is, confined and treated by experienced medical practitioners. Many would be redeemed if removed from temptation, and the will to indulge in strong drink has been hemmed in. Much misery would thereby be wiped out, and millions of dollars left in the possession of those to whom it originally belonged. A drunken man is often far more dangerous than the insane human being; why, then, should not society protect itself from such vice by bringing them under control of the law, without distinction, rich and poor, high and low, receiving a similar treatment? Private institutions have shown the benefit in this overshadowing vice of your nation; therefore to make it more general in the United States, and in fact all civilized countries, a law should be enacted which would secure the patient at proper places until cured. This also may be applied to opium smoking, another detested vice fast growing into use in your State, and in fact the United States.

"To proceed with our subject, in giving the history of the two beings in this cell I mentioned that the temperance man was not a temperate man, but in this contest with the drunkard, in this thought-battle, he must come out victorious over the drunkard, whose rough exterior, as two rough diamonds, when rubbed and crushed together one is worn the most, or when applied to the soul, one is benefited the most by its own suffering. In the coming period, the occupants of the cell are changed; one is brought to bear his thoughts upon the temperance man by one who was temperate in the uses of other luxuries or necessities in life, and then the temperance man receives the brunt and is humiliated and reminded that he was, after all, not so perfect as his egotism had caused him to think. Thus we work one sin, one gross passion, against the virtue of another soul, although that soul may be deficient in another point of perfection also. Before us none arrive who are so pure that no deficiency is noticed which clings to the character of their soul; but not only do we see the faults and sins, the ignoble passions which have ruled them while passing their allotted time below, but their virtues, good deeds, and self-control they exercised over themselves in a ruling passion, are equally known, and by this knowledge we strive to do our grinding in the polishing of the souls under our care.

"You will perceive from this that the primary work of the polishing process is to work sinner against sinner, one, however, being a less sinner in certain crimes than another. No human being is so perfect as not to have some vice attached, some ruling passion which has tunneled and drilled itself into the soul, living with it as a parasite. The most despised and abhorred criminal in your penitentiary often possesses virtues which the reported good man may lack, and which would almost make him be deserving the good name he carries. God, who judges the criminal, so-called, because his criminality has been discovered or he was not enabled to establish his innocence, with you, must atone for the crime right or wrong. With us, neither one nor the other is wanting in the faults and sins that cling to the human soul on its arrival here, and these deficiencies must be erased, the dark spots washed out, the soul made pure and fit for the high station it is to occupy. Your doctrines below would have us believe, that because a man has lived according to your codes of law; that because a man has done some good to mankind; went to church regularly, and looked upon God as a low Chinaman does when in presence of a high Mandarin, or a slave to his master; that the soul of such man or woman may jump into the center of heaven like a clown into the middle of the circus ring, crying out, 'I am here.' The laws of heaven are not formulated thus.

"In your world below knowledge cannot be poured through a funnel into your brain. It must be gained by constant attention and labor of the mind; often the limbs are necessary also to educate the whole for the branch to which the human being has devoted himself or herself. Your reputed scientist, inventor, literary man, composer and general who has gained the fame of being a genius, will be found upon closer investigation to have been more of a worker and systematic observer, than a genius who has fallen out of the clouds ready made to order, as the word appears to imply. You must not comprehend from this that I deny that man is born with certain faculties adapting him specially for certain studies, enterprises or work. It is, however, frequently the case when nature lavishly furnishes certain recesses of the brain, when she bestows more substance upon certain faculties of man, she does it at the expense of other faculties, or in other words, when the vigor of the mind in one direction is more than usually vigorous, it is frequently the case that it is greatly diminished in another, and in all such cases there must follow some deficiency in judgment. For instance, a man may be noted as a musical genius and at the same time represent an idiot. As I have stated that with you it requires a will to propel yourself forward intellectually, so it still does up here to bring you to a higher state, and without your energy and will you cannot advance.

VICE AND VIRTUE HARNESSED TOGETHER.

"We will stop at this cell, Mr. Smith, where two females have been placed not many hours ago. You see one is old, the other less than twenty years of age.

"And very beautiful," I added.

"It is true," he replied; "the very cause that the grain did not ripen for the sickle, that she came before her time, or rather that she did not reach the usual age nature fitted up her human frame to exist in your world. The girl was murdered by her lover. She was one of those unfortunates who had sold her virtue for money. Flattery was one of the causes that resulted in her ruin. Flattery against vanity, and vanity fell; and being down, friend and foe trampled upon vanity and she could never redeem herself again. Do you know, in no country in your wide world is a woman held lower, who follows her occupation, than in yours. Such a woman is meant to be forever cut off from all that has a tendency to improve mankind religiously. Did He whom you place at the head of your great Christian religion act on that Pharasaical principle? Was He ashamed to be seen with them? Did He utterly condemn them? Is it the greatest crime that a woman can follow, and is it entirely impossible to redeem that class from their evil doings? By the scorn and indifference, the reception they receive everywhere, and most by their own sex, they must fall lower.

"There are noble women in other countries of large cities, who do not think themselves defiled in their efforts to lead them to a better life, when their dress comes in contact with theirs. Many of these girls would be redeemed if only an effort were made by some noble and high-minded woman, with influence and high standing. Such an one would receive recruits in her ranks despite the moral courage it requires.

"Even if such a girl could not return to her parents, who frequently are occupying social positions, she could at least be made self-sustaining by honest labor, under the supervision of matrons appointed for the position, and when redeemed she may become yet a useful member of society. There ought to be a woman society extending over your broad land, whose duty it should be to elevate that class of females. Is it any greater shame to redeem a fallen woman than an intemperate man? Do not the Good Templars and similar societies take in their ranks both sexes equally? Is it less a good deed before God and man to save a woman by woman than a man by woman? In spite of your reforms and your advance, both the drunkard and the woman of easy virtue you will always have amongst you, but their number could be reduced by adopting more humane and christian treatment. Christianity preached from pulpits and christianity actually carried out works quite differently.

"You judge the crimes below committed against society, but you seldom know, or care to inquire into the causes. We know the circumstances, and judge accordingly, up here. The greatest sin may lose much of its horror were all matters connected with it fully known to you; but let me acquaint you further with the character of the two occupants before us. The girl was stabbed to death by one of her lovers while raging under an attack of jealousy, and here is the soul to atone for the sins she committed. The old lady led a strictly virtuous life, so far as men were concerned; for being crossed in love early, or rather, finding her lover untrue to her, making use of one of the class just mentioned, she broke the engagement, and forever hated those unfortunate women, and men, too, in general.

"This woman was very wealthy, and had the means and will to do considerable good in the way of charity. She cheerfully gave to the poor, seldom making inquiries how her money was applied. She kept and fed whole families, who otherwise would have rendered honest service to the world, but by her charities they remained paupers, idlers, hypocrites and frauds, using the surplus money for intemperate purposes and luxuries to which such people are not entitled.

"It often happens that benevolent or charitable people, when they supply a human being with money, think they have carried out a Christian act, and such is frequently the case when the gift is actually required by an extremely impoverished individual. It is oftener the case, however, that the person in need would have been much better served morally, if supplied with work, and the work furnished paid for. To keep your impoverished people in money and food you cause them to despise labor, and love idleness and intemperance. Had this woman really spent her money judiciously for the poor, by giving honest employment, many just such girls would have been kept out of houses in which her present companion passed part of her ill-spent life. She directly, even, was the cause of girls seeking quarters in such places, simply because the families under her protection kept their children in idleness, and brought them up to intemperance.

VIEWS ABOUT LABOR.

"Honest labor is appreciated with us; idleness does much mischief. Every young man and woman, rich or poor, ought to be brought up —compulsory, if necessary—to do some manual labor, or learn a trade. The wealth the parents possess often takes wings, and the young man or woman known as GENTLEMAN and LADY, who have not had instruction in any manual labor, or were ashamed to perform any, find themselves in a condition worse than servants. Education and cultivation, by all means; but do not neglect the trades and mechanical labor ever necessary in civilized life. The woman who has been so fortunate as to have been born of rich and indulgent parents, who expended their thousands to bring the girl's education up to the highest standard, giving her what is termed a 'finished education,' may yet think herself unfortunate that her parents thought it of no importance to have her instructed in the arts of the kitchen and the household. It is there where your true woman shines; it is there where she ought to rule, and it is not absolutely necessary that much labor should be performed by herself. What is wanted is to know how the work should be carried out. Thousands of unhappy marriages and divorces are caused every year on account of this deficiency.

"Cookery ought to be looked upon as an art, and instructions ought to be given all over the land to young women. Every city ought to possess its famous cooking schools, and be as proud of its laboratory as of a conservatory of music, and even more so, as you can exist, if need be, without music, but all mortals must eat and drink, and why not train your coming generations to produce only that which is most palatable and wholesome for them?

HINTS TO THE WEALTHY.

"Your rich can aid much in bringing the lower classes up to some useful occupation. The little boy and girl, properly employed, will in a short time be self-sustaining. The man who sets in motion so many young and nimble hands with his money, starting a new industry which had to rely upon European or Asiatic countries, retains the money in your country and becomes a benefactor to the employed. A man of wealth may give one hundred thousand dollars to a university fund and carry out a good act. Another rich man takes the same amount from his surplus funds and builds a small factory, where he keeps fifty or a hundred girls and boys employed and instructed in useful occupations, adapted to their sex. Out of the two, the one who gave the labor is likely to cause the most good to the poor. But even labor must be systematically performed, and science and art everywhere should be the guide. Any mechanic of note who is deficient in drawing, necessary mathematical knowledge, and similar aids in the work he is engaged in, must be kept in the background. Therefore, the man who sets his forty to fifty boys to work must not expect them to work like clocks or steam engines set in motion, but he must also aid them by intellectual instructions, or else your workers will be mere machines. Man, in future, must act as the guide; the forces of nature, which his mind has learned him to harness, will produce the muscles and sinews. The spirit and mind of the machine must ever be the man himself. Every State ought to possess its technical schools, which in fact have become an absolute necessity in the older countries, and if you intend to keep step with the world, your rich men may there show some true benevolence in bringing the masses upward, combining labor with useful knowledge necessary for the work.

"But not too much reliance should be placed in such hopes, as it has been proved that all your millionaires dying the past twenty years, have done little or nothing to return some of their wealth from whence it originally came, or to a large extent. Particularly were the so-termed good church members noted for letting all the almighty dollars gathered in a lifetime and stored in one corner, be divided amongst the already rich relatives. A few known as 'cranks,' who had the boldness to act differently, gave an opportunity for fat slices to the lawyers. If your rich man really wants to do anything for the future in your world, he must not intrust such work to his relatives and friends. He must be his own supervisor and dispenser, and with the aid of professional men he can carry through any project he may entertain to set in motion. The Government and State should become interested. It is far better to instruct your boys in schools of that description and have them acquire occupations, than to have them years after learn some trade in a penitentiary. The mind of the child ought to be prepared as early as possible for it, looking upon work as play, and in this the disciples of Frœbel come into place or play. In their instructions to the young mind, the child, without knowing or undergoing forced study, acquires knowledge, and that through its play or work as you may choose to term it. The soft clay in the hands of a child may already show by its molding, that from this boy may be made a second Phidias or a Powers, and it is thus in other branches of the arts and trades.

"But to return to our two souls, one known as a virtuous woman and benevolent, the other as one who had followed vice and thereby doing herself more harm than others. The misapplication of the elder woman's benevolence and charity has been explained to you, and you will admit it has caused more harm than benefit, but she meant the latter, giving considerable honey with a great deal of rank poison. These two souls are now in position; the main work to be accomplished for the present is by the elder upon the younger, making clear her wrong doings, and causing repentance and a will to atone for it, paying attention to the progressive rules necessary. In the next change the elder lady will come in contact with a spirit who has caused some good work to be done, without boasting, as an act of charity; it was carried out without the aid of much money, but rather by giving useful instructions and by thus placing honest and ready capital at hand for the aided, to use in future, and thereby become self-sustaining. The old lady will then come to recognize her much esteemed charitable acts to have been far less beneficial than she thought them to be to enter the little gate St. Peter has ready as a reward, but allows so very few to pass through.

"You see all along here on both sides you find souls in torture by virtues and vices being harnessed together, and the primary work is to match great virtues over predominating vices, and as every human being is noted to have performed some good deeds, the soul is entitled to work upon its opposite as a reformer, and in such cases your greatest criminal may become the teacher of the better soul. When gradually the grosser sins have been obliterated by the working virtues of another, then our work begins for higher preparations. We may speak of that further on, if time permits.

PHILOSOPHER AND HORSE JOCKEY.

"Here, Mr. Smith, are two interesting subjects. Satisfy your curiosity well, if you entertain any."

"I think they are rather opposite in their intellect, one appearing as having been educated, while the other shows little or no traces excepting a sort of low cunning, sometimes denominated smartness," I answered, after my survey of the two.

"Quite right; you read character excellently, so far as the exterior is concerned. Of course their history is not known or what they really represented below. Had we near us the shades of La Vater, he could explain to you the differences of their physiognomies and what the parts indicate, when thus and thus formed or placed. The shades of Gall and Spurzheim could give you further points as to their intellect, by the examination of the shape of their heads. I pretend to be learned in a few, but my specialty is to read the soul itself and its history, and all the arts and the sciences of your little world below will never possess that knowledge, it never being intended to arm man with such power below.

"We will proceed. The large man with massive head and deep sunken eyes, appearing as if in deep study, or peering into the mysteries of the future, was a great scientist and philosopher; a giant amongst the learned; a Newton and Humboldt in spirit, and a man who accomplished a vast amount of mental labor, making discoveries and causing inventions by which many men have grown wealthy, while he himself had not thought to protect his work, as it is now done, by taking out patents, or protecting your own brain labor. This man only worked for the general benefit of man, or the love of knowledge, and, as is the usual case, he died comparatively poor. In his search through Nature he did not meet a God, or a Ruling Spirit. He gave all his credit to Nature herself, acknowledging neither God, a soul, or a life beyond.

"The small man, with short hair, low forehead, quick-moving monkey eyes, flat nose, with open, large nostrils, and big mouth with retreating chin, and short, bull-like neck, was a horse jockey, who died rich, and believing in a Supreme Being. Dishonesty was his ruling passion; so his acquired wealth, although not stolen, was yet acquired by low trickery, to which the nobler character of the philosopher would never stoop, and yet here the jockey is placed above the philosopher, in order to humiliate him, and to find his hell with a character he from his boyhood despised and abhorred. In the contest of thoughts going on between them regarding a Supreme Being, the less learned soul has the advantage. His simple answers and questions are short, but to the point, and in course of time the giant in intellect will find himself routed by the soul of a simple-minded mortal, while he himself soared with the celestial bodies, and calculated their revolutions around the sun while in life. This confinement and humiliation that one spirit must accept from the other, is a greater hell, producing incalculably more pain than any torture that can be inflicted upon man physically. But even with you, mental pain produces greater changes than when the body is subjected to torture. Thus the revolving wheel, representing the soul of a horse jockey who believed in a Supreme Being, is made to grind off the rough coating of a most valuable diamond, or a disbelieving philosopher is taught by one far below his knowledge to acknowledge a Greater Power than Nature herself. In their progress, as in the world below, the advantages are with the learned after his prejudices and predominating sin are removed. Those learned in Nature have already taken initiatory steps to progress. Everywhere the change is to advance and be moving—no idleness, no standing still, ever acquiring the knowledge to rise higher and higher, and in this, so far as the natural laws extend, the man of science has already served some apprenticeship; but he must be made to acknowledge, must himself be convinced, that there is some power greater than Nature, and that Nature simply represents the scenery; that the Almighty is the sceneshifter, and artist too.

CATHOLIC, PROTESTANT AND JEW.

"In this cell you find a Catholic and a Protestant, of common order and intelligence, each proclaiming his religion THE BEST. Both are right, and wrong, too. The next you find the same, of a higher order, and the arguments in thought are here more refined, more theoretical and argumentative, but the substance is the same. Both will advance more rapidly than the other two, who are less intelligent, after they have acquired the true knowledge to advancement, for the training of the soul below gives it great advantage here.

"In this cell there are placed a Jew and Mohammedan, and in the opposite one, a Christian and Jew. Both pairs are of a lower order, but in the next cell you find a Catholic priest and a rabbi belaboring each other intellectually, and this is a sharp contest, and about even. The rabbi, or older religion, the foundation of the Christian religion itself, is too much for the priest, who finds himself, with all his learning, vanquished by the Jew; but were they to oppose each other for the good actions rendered in general to mankind, the priest's good deeds, in this case, at least, would outweigh the rabbi's; but this is not intended here, as I perceive from the arrangement. This is only a little contest between religions, to wear off the rough coatings by friction, and the priest's exterior must be roughly scratched to lay bare the glittering diamond within. The Jew will be attacked at a different point, where he is found vulnerable. I assure you we have their hell for all of them; but their pain improves their characters and beings, while below it often causes the human devils only to sink lower and lower. Do you not call this improvement?

"Frequently we bring the bigoted Christian, Jew, Mohammedan, and other religions acknowledging a God, in contact with each other, in order to take out the conceit they imbibed while in life. It is quite necessary to take out their conceit, for they can never banish the thought that their religion is not the best, but in worshiping, even to the Deity, and nothing more, lies not salvation alone. But by their works we know them—not the professions they make in behalf of their religion."

ADVANCEMENT.

We had by this time advanced to a considerable distance in one direction, and soon a slight alteration in architecture took place; the arching of the roofs became higher, the doors of the cell larger, and the cells also more comfortable, larger aud lighter. After walking some distance in this new division, he remarked:

"I will now give you some idea of spirits somewhat more advanced in this reformatory. Look into this room and you will perceive a group of twelve, representing a number of religions and nationalities. They are of both sexes, as you see, but sometimes the sexes only meet; and let me inform you, until some advance is made, that is, when the passions have been expelled which had taken possession of that soul while on earth, not until then are the sexes mixed. If you could read their countenances as readily as I am enabled to, you would perceive a great change between the first souls and those here. But even YOUR eyes notice some change. They are now interchanging thoughts; they compare each other's faults and deficiencies; some will defend them for a while, but finally find themselves vanquished and will yield. Every meeting brings favorable results, for it has become much easier to overcome obstacles. The spirit is now on its progressive passage, and MUST advance. There are very many, many things to acquire, but it would be useless to inform you of them, since you cannot understand them, nor can the new comers. The comparison is greater than this: You endeavor to to teach a child the alphabet, and having acquired a few letters you introduce choice readings, that only highly educated persons could fully comprehend. You teach a child to count, and then bring forward some mathematical problem, with algebraical formulas and calculations. Now, what benefit would be bestowed upon the child in proceeding thus? There must be gradations here, as with you below; the mind, so to say, of the soul must comprehend before it enters higher stations. The theory with you being that all who enter hell must undergo torture, and as they are intended to be there forever and ever the torture and beings increasing in pain and wickedness. I will put it differently: In a box there is found one bad apple, with several hundred others; out of these, by some law of nature, one has become rotten and at a certain stage of the disease attacks its neighbor, and so one another until the whole box is affected. Just so in hell in the end, as the devils are the greatest enemies of God so would all the souls become toward the last.

"In society it is frequently the case that one bad man, one bad woman, make others similar, and the number increases in mathematical progression—2, 4, 8, 16, 32, etc. The majority naturally must have considerable influence upon the minor or a single person. Say you take one of your most abandoned cow-boys of the far West and put him at the table with a dozen refined gentlemen of Boston or New York. You clothe your half savage similar to his associates and treat him similar in every respect as you do the others. Do you think the fellow would then act in the same manner as he would with his own associates? Continue this process and give him other opportunities, and you may make some sort of a so-called gentleman out of him, or he may even surpass them, if he had any education previously. Now take one of your fine gentlemen, pack him amongst a lot of twenty or thirty cow-boys, cut-throats and thieves; let him associate from day to day with them, and even if he has remained upright and honest, he will have lost much of the gentleman and acquired bad manners.

"This the child does from beginning, born of savage or civilized parents. Man imitates from the time his senses begin to develop, and it extends beyond. We therefore at the beginning bring only the good to bear upon him, or for every vice we have a virtue to oppose until the vice is wiped out. And thus the process continues at every point. It is hoped you understand the philosophy of the treatment. Our process or method would consequently have a tendency to continue in improvement or to make better and better, entering station after station, glory after glory, until he may reach the highest honors. If the 'Ruler' contemplated you to be damned forever because you could not be perfect in all things, it were better not to have been created man; but he intended that all must rise higher, but the advance must be by their own energy, just the same as below mentally, where it is impossible to improve the mind unless one makes an effort.

"It is true religionists tell you that to be saved all that is necessary is to have strong faith. But do you call it rational for an investigating creature like man to take it for granted because this man and the other man said so? If God gifted man with reasoning power, He must permit him investigation, or reasoning could not be of any benefit. Blind faith simply signifies worse than slavery. The Deity intended man to be self-sustaining, and all he has thus far accomplished was through his own investigations and experiments. It is all nonsense to caution you against this and that, for it belongs to his own sphere; all, all is yours if the giant mind of some man can comprehend it, and not only what you may find in your own world, but your mind is at liberty to soar far above, revolving and traversing bodies millions of miles away from your earth. Superstition has done a great deal to retard the progress of nations, and much undeserved praise and reward was often bestowed upon quacks and charletans who were forever ready to exhibit their dark doings with the 'Bad One,' as they pretended. Now science wants the field clear. Natural philosophy clears up many great mysteries regarding nature, and lies and falsehoods are now stamped into the ground. There must be truth in an assertion, because now investigators are too many who have drank from the fountain of nature's laws. When, however, it comes to the forces of the soul, and the relation it bears towards the body, comparatively little progress has been made, and yet the past and present furnishes much to speculate upon.

PSYCHOLOGY.

"Psychology is in its infancy yet; in fact, it is frequently entirely ignored by some of your learned men, who entertain a dislike towards it, showing their prejudice whenever an opportunity is offered, and yet they are not enabled to clear up certain mysteries with which almost any medical practitioner comes in contact during a lifetime, yet many of those learned and scientific gentlemen ignore the soul. If none, why this craving for knowledge, not only to accumulate wealth, but to comprehend the wise laws of Nature that everywhere, to the thinking human being, manifest themselves. In the late transit of Venus the accurate calculations of the ancient makers of the Strasbourg clock proved true. These calculations were made by Conrad Dasypobius between 1571-4—over three hundred years ago. A few days before the transit occurred, visitors to the cathedral, inspecting the planetarium attached to the clock, noticed that one of the small gilt balls, representing Venus, was gradually moving towards a point between the sun and the earth and on the day of the passage the ball stood exactly between them. Why should the knowledge exist to 'create' such a clock—giving its due proportion to both maker and calculator—if nothing greater was to come when human life is ended upon your planet?

"Then there is another class that have sprung up in this century, or within thirty years, more or less, who attribute all this force to the spirits in other worlds. I will not go into this study deeper at present, but may probably refer to it once more before we part, when some points may be given to interest you, although the benefit perhaps all lies in awakening curiosity. It is hardly possible the world will become wiser for it. All you gain in your advancement below and up here, must come by your own energy alone. Wise men and women are only produced thus, and perfect spirits must keep step, in a spiritual sense, on the same principle.

"You may now view several more of the rooms, with their occupants, about here. In this one you find a group of twelve, who are females. They are from early age, up to almost a lifetime of one century. They are advanced spirits, as all are about here, consequently permitted, or in a spiritual condition, to commingle with the other sex; but this meeting is devoted principally to their sex, and certain branches of studies they are connected with.

"We will pay attention to one more being of importance about here. This door, as you perceive, is considerably larger than others.

It is the entrance to a small hall, seating about five hundred persons, in your world; they can place many more should it become necessary, but at present if you lift the wicket you will only find about that number represented. There is a small stage or rostrum where the master of ceremonies or president of the assembly has his seat. You will at once notice he is not one of them, but belongs to a higher class of souls or beings. He is, in fact, one of those created prior to man, and not on your earth. He belongs to my species, but somewhat later—a few hundred years with us is but a trifle as regards time, you know. He acts as teacher and instructor in the branch they are engaged in at present, and the time they are kept together is about equivalent to one hour below, which here is a rather brief time. But the duties are so varied that no branch on the onward march can be neglected."

We then continued to walk another stretch, when he remarked: "We have now advanced quite a distance into the northern part of this palace. I only selected the few abodes and meeting places to give you variety, and opportunity to form some idea, also to impress upon your mind to keep in memory on your return below. You may rest assured all the doors of the rooms and cells you passed, through the passages, contained soul-occupants, and bear in mind there are thousands of passages radiating in every direction, about which the same can truthfully be said, and these passages extend for miles and miles into the interior. This vast home of departed souls must necessarily be large and spacious to hold generation after generation of human beings. With the cast-off shell left below, the law is different; nature remolds and recasts again and brings forth new forms. The atoms which once formed a beautiful woman may be found next in a drop of dew or an icicle, or it may be in the body of a loathsome reptile; it may be found in a poison plant or the most fragrant and beautiful flower. The whole proceeding is like one of those curious kaleidescopes which by every shake produces different forms of crystalization."

HUMAN BODY ASSUMING NEW FORM.

"But is this really true, Mr. Lucifer?" I inquired.

"True, Mr. Smith? Why, Mr. Smith, this little knowledge many a school boy acquires now-a-days, but if you do not comprehend the statement made, I will explain the matter more minutely still," he answered, and he went on explaining the process of nature thus: "If your body, left in charge of your friends below, is not reoccupied by the soul, it must necessarily die and be decomposed, signifying to disunite the elementary particles combined by affinity or attraction, to resolve themselves into their original elements. The gases of hydrogen and oxygen, when combined by being two atoms of the first with one of the last gas, forms water (H O), and the animal as well as the human being contains about seventy-five per cent. of water. In order to impress upon your mind, it must be made clear to you that according to the law of chemistry a body may be destroyed; changing its original form, and yet the elements cannot be destroyed, the atoms simply change, forming other or new compounds. Thus if water, for instance, were decomposed by electric action or otherwise, the gases, or one of the gases, according to the methods adopted, are simply separated and can take new form. The hydrogen and oxygen may combine with another element, forming a new compound. In our case it is not even necessary that the two gases, hydrogen and oxygen, forming water, should be separated, as there is an agent which separates the water from the body direct. The decomposition also depends upon the method adopted, particularly the agent that plays an important part in forming various compounds as the body is decomposed. If cremation were adopted, for instance, the elements would return to nature at once and produce new forms. We will first admit that a simple process like evaporation reduces the body, dries it up or mummifies it to the amount of seventy-five per cent. The water has evaporated, the molecules of water, as vapor, minutely divided and subdivided, are held in suspension in the air. The copartnership existing which formerly held a certain quantity of water in one body has been gradually dissolved by slow evaporation, and the wind and storms may have carried the now suspended vapor around the globe. Here and there, by the laws of nature, the vapors are condensed to water, and are precipitated as rain, snow or dew. One of these minute quantities, emanating from the destroyed body, may find its way into a spring and be drank by a human Venus who rests near there, or the most hideous or ferocious animal may come to drink at the same place and take another subdivided part of the liquid. Some part of it may find its way to some plant which bears luscious fruit; the root takes up the atom and carries it through the trunk and its divisions until it finds its way into one of the luscious fruits which a modern Adam plucks to give to his Eve, who next possesses it. By a kiss subsequently given by Eve to Adam, a part may become evaporated from her lips and in the breathing process of Adam the subdivided atom has been appropriated and probably not retained long, as your modern Adams generally are very gallant and return such compliments immediately, particularly if the Eve bears any resemblance to the first woman regarding beauty. Thus the atom may for a while fly from place to place, like a bee or bird of paradise from flower to flower gathering honey. You can imagine, and think out yourself the changes that can occur simply through evaporation alone. If, on the other hand, the water was decomposed, as probably some portion would be in cremating the body, the hydrogen would have combined with the nitrogen in the air, and by electrical aid converted the two gases into the gas known as ammonium which would be appropriated by the precipitated drops in its passage through the air, coming down with the rain water. This rain water may next assist to furnish nutriment to plant life, the ammonia then in small quantities acting to the plant as the phosphates in food for the animal. The liberated oxygen, if pure as such, could immediately be used again as in breathing, or in the combustion of fuel, or oxidation in general, and in such cases the product would be carbonic acid, which nature furnishes to the plant to draw its carbon from, aided by the light of the sun (or even electric light). In other words, the carbonic acid is again decomposed, the leaves of the plant or tree withdrawing the carbon to store up for itself by the aid of light. The oxygen is given back, the carbon is in the tree, and part again may be found in the wood or the sugar of the fruit as nature has willed.

"Now when we take the less material, the earthy matter of the body, the reduced ashes, phosphate of lime, magnesia, silica, iron, etc., this can all be used again for plant life, and from the fruit and plant, man and the animals take into their systems the same elements furnished by man or animal first. These are fixed laws of Nature, taking place continually, but thought of by few. After acquiring this knowledge of man, both regarding soul and body, does it not seem insipid to read on your monuments raised over your dead, 'Eternal Rest.'? Where is eternal rest to be found? Ever moving, ever going, ever doing, are the laws of Nature—no absolute standing still; and here you see this process is still continued with your soul, and all, all by the divine wisdom of Him who rules the universe."

We had by this time arrived at a large open space, and Lucifer remarked: "I have in my enthusiasm overlooked showing you one or more large halls. We have passed a door leading to one which has a seating capacity of over ten thousand souls. It is generally the case when I am enlarging upon the wise laws of Nature, and the higher spiritual laws of Him from whom all has sprung, I am forgetting my own station. I only think how I can magnify Him most who is above us all."

"As you are intended to return below," Lucifer continued, "it may not be out of place to say a few words regarding your young nation. We will select those seats in the centre of this station, where we will have a better view of the surroundings when the time arrives."

AMERICAN POLITICS.

By this time we had arrived and seated ourselves, and he continued: "Your nation is quite young yet in the world's history, and if wise men were selected, they would keep clear of the quicksands into which you may plunge, and where every effort is used to extract yourself, you will only sink deeper. Older nations have made grave mistakes in their history, and those mistakes the historian noted down for the wise to profit by. The remedy should be applied before the disease has attacked, or made its appearance. In the countries of older nations, generally men are appointed, or elected, who are fitted for their positions, which, I am sorry to say, is not always the case with you. When an office is held by a man, he must have qualified himself for the position, otherwise he will make a poor representative. With you, political trickery, the love of office, and the almighty lever, money, hoists many an incapable quack and imposter into office, to which neither his intelligence nor patriotism had any claim.

"This state of affairs will continue for some time yet in the newer States and Territories. In the older States there is not the slightest reason to elect men to any office to which they are not fitted. In both the great parties material may be found which would be satisfactory, as far as capability and loyalty are concerned; but generally such men are not of the sort who go about begging for office, although not being incumbered with more of worldly goods than their neighbors, who have courage, or 'brass,' as you call it sometimes, but less ability, or not any at all. What's the difference? Cannot a man be found to carry out the real brain work? Often the real personage of an office is a subordinate who has for a number of years occupied his position, mastering the situation with which he was intrusted. Generally, such men rise no higher, although they may write and furnish the brains for the speeches of the so-called 'great men' who have climbed the political ladder round after round. Such a man besides, fills his purse, while the really deserving remains stationary. The tricky and ignorant politician, native or foreign born, steps higher, and grows fat in wealth with his family. The worthy man is barely enabled to rear his family respectably with the salary he receives, and all about him, in contact with such upstarts, he is made to feel his subordinate position. There is, indeed, a great deal to perform by both of your great parties that rule the republic at present.

"There are several reforms which have to be carried out sooner or later. I will speak plainer, and say the tolerence of arming your ignorant men by permitting them to vote upon all questions I consider wrong. It is doubly wrong, because your laws debar those often possessed of more intelligence and property. In an intelligent republic like the United States of North America, there ought not in the year of our Lord eighteen hundred and eighty-two be over six millions of people who are unable to read and write. Yet every one of those ignoramuses, it matters little be he native or foreign born, if he has acquired citizenship, can eliminate or neutralize the vote of an intelligent citizen who has acquired the knowledge regarding the question to be voted on, while the other has learned all through hearsay. An American born man, white, black, or yellow, who has not at this age had sufficient ambition to learn to read and write, or whose parents were so ignorant and stupid as to let their children be brought up without this necessary education, ought to be deprived of the franchise until they have acquired this necessary knowledge. The same may be applied to the foreigner, if at the end of five years he has not acquired sufficient of the English language to know at least how to read and what he is voting about. In both cases there should be, at the proper time or first permission to vote, some examination regarding American history and some of the principal laws governing the country. A man entitled to vote ought to have sufficient intelligence to know at least how the General Government and State is ruled. Such an examination should become a law, for then many would make an effort to gain the requisite knowledge.

FEMALE SUFFRAGE.

"We, who know the sexes well enough to judge them correctly, think it judicious to include all intelligent females of proper age. Many of those are even superior in intelligence to their fathers, husbands, and brothers, having acquired far better educations, and frequently they represent a large amount of property too, which they have learned to manage and superintend, surpassing their relatives or men generally, whose wives and daughters they represent. The idea held that woman is unfit for certain stations, because she is a woman, is a great mistake. Frequently the whole management of a family is in the woman alone, the husband representing the figurehead simply. Now compare this law or custom, which allows an ignorant person, of no property perhaps, to vote upon all questions, while a woman, naturally fitted from youth up for business and representing thousands of dollars in property is deprived of this right in behalf of her own. We will submit one case in behalf of the intelligent female, also representing property. Say a lady has been well brought up, receiving an excellent education in her youth, and circumstances compelled her to take charge of her father's property, he being an invalid. Being naturally shrewd and having, in course of time, acquired business knowledge besides, she learned to manage the estate, amounting from one hundred and fifty thousand dollars to two hundred thousand dollars, as well as any business man in town where she resides and was born. Then imagine a corporation that requires four hundred to five hundred additional ordinary laborers, which they employ ; and in the meantime the company asks certain privileges from the city which, however, would be equivalent to additional taxation upon the property holder. When election day arrives, every one of the five hundred laborers, not representing one dollar in real estate, and many of them unable to read and write, can be made to vote and thereby force that woman to pay a large amount of taxes which she knows is without the slightest financial benefit to herself. Here the intelligent woman, representing a large amount of property, has not a word to say in protecting herself, while the ignorant laborer, without a foot of real estate, represents one of your boasted sovereigns. Is this just and honest? Can this ever remain thus? It is an easy matter to vote other people's money away when one has nothing. In such cases, a man representing no property should not be permitted to vote when it is necessary to levy extra taxation, excepting for school purposes, which must ever be free to all. The older nations of Europe allow a citizen to vote upon matters concerning the country at large, but prevent such a person from exercising the same right in town matters in the town where he resides, unless he represents property, and the citizens themselves have given him permission, or permitted him citizenship of the town also.

DANGER TO THE REPUBLIC.

"This is one of the questions of considerable importance, for upon the lower class and the extremely rich depends the future of the republic. The danger lies in the powerful lever—money, which your over-rich men may throw out as a bait to accomplish their end. Considerable has been said and written about the influence of foreigners, who have made their homes in your country in such large numbers. It is feared they will revolutionize the country. The Irish and German are feared, being the greater representatives of foreigners. Inquire of these people what brought them here, and they may give various reasons; all know, however, that they intend to remain and make their home in your republic, and although they may still love their native country, they would not favor a monarchy being established here, and would prefer to shed their blood against its principles if an attempt be made. The majority of both these nationalities, during your 'brotherly contest' some time ago, if my memory serves me right, threw their weight in the Northern balance of the scale, which finally bore down the Southern brother. Their blood and property was sacrificed for the cause, equal to the native born in proportion to numbers. Had the contest been favorable to the Southern brother, which meant a dismembering of the 'American Union,' who knows but some monarch might now have something to say in your country.

"Think not that a great nation, whose government is republican, and who has grown in one century to such great power and large proportion, which has made such giant strides in the arts and industries or general advancement, and to whom the whole civilized world looks when its people feel themselves oppressed—think not that all the pretensions of love and good will are the genuine article. Nations, like individuals, will bear envy and jealousy, and no individual yet born of low origin and risen to power and strength, has had the good fortune or ability not to cause these feelings in those lower in rank. Men sprung from the lowest class, who have attained the highest rank, have not generally had their paths upward strewn with roses and other fragrant flowers—few roses, but many thorns.

"There may be such profession of friendship by some European nations, whose government is represented by a monarchy, but the friendship is not to be wholly trusted, when judging from the experience gained about twenty years ago. It says plainly, 'I would like to have you low-born churl out of the way, but your great strength hinders me from having you humiliated and vanquished.' This is about the love some monarchs of Europe entertain for you at present, have in the past, and will in the future.

"As far as the safety of the Republic is concerned within, the rich directly bear against it. When a man from the lower ranks has acquired his millions, of course always by honest means, for you punish all wrong doings, as your penitentiaries show, where you put all such men who pilfer, steal, rob and sometimes murder, if they have no friends and no 'almighty dollars' about them to assist them in procuring HONEST counselors, who interest themselves in the justice of the case with which they are charged. If the man with millions should make any of the above mistakes, he would probably find a way which would not compel him to reside behind iron doors with big locks and bolts attached, as auxiliary safety charms.

"Now your aristocracy is not of noble birth, cannot date back and point to its illustrious ancestors fighting in a thousand battles, or having made so many thousand mortals happy or miserable. What do they care about their ancestors and their names? Is it not known that they are frequently ashamed of the very name which became attached to them at their birth, and have they not frequently changed their names or modernized them? If some blue blood, however, ever flowed in the veins of their forefathers, the world will probably be made aware of it. But that is human nature. This is not launched at your nation alone—the thing is general enough below, to claim rich and influential relatives. The old gentleman, once Prime Minister of France, and who receives his training here at present, might give you some information on the subject; and in your country, where they are more grateful, the elevated ones make all their relatives happy by apportioning some lucrative office, according to the love they bear them or the service rendered. So we are informed.

"Generally your 'money-bag,' also often termed 'self-made man,' cares neither for ancestors or the past. He points with pride to his millions of accumulated wealth. He is shrewd enough to have learned that even the bluest of the blue blood of the noblest and most illustrious houses of Europe also bow down (they often must) to worship the golden calf, or probably the golden bull. If the self made man, oftener the wife and daughters of the self-made man, visit Europe, they will, when they become known in the various countries they visit, everywhere attract the younger and stronger sex of the blue-blood society, who find themselves attracted to your republican daughters (despite their low origin), as flies are attracted by honey and sweetmeats. In short, the high-born noble of Europe makes love to the plain republican daughter and the expected portion of money-bags, and as the daughter of the 'self-made man' has been brought up according to aristocratic principles. she desires to soar in that sphere, and now the opportunity is offered and accepted too. One offers at the shrine of love an ancestry of one thousand years, with all its honors—principally in the past. The income must be drawn from the Jews who have long ago taken possession of all family estates. The other offers her beauty, American principles, and what old 'self-made man' is made to disgorge of his wealth, and then the happiness of married life begins. The ambitious daughter, and mother-in-law even, may find themselves in the holy of holies, and glory of glories, by being permitted to kiss the hand of some royal personage or be honored by breathing the atmosphere in close proximity to them, at some noted royal gathering, If the young American noblese is handsome and clever, as most of them are, she may even have bestowed upon her some flattering remarks about her nation and herself.

COMING NOBILITY.

"Impress this upon your mind, Mr. Smith. Reflect; look into the future; what does this prophesy? Why must this rich woman of low origin, reared in a republican country, attach herself and relatives to the house of a noble family residing in a monarchy? Are there not handsome, well educated and wealthy young men in your own country, frequently too with more vigor and energy than the scion of a defunct nobility?

"Then there is another straw showing from what direction the wind blows. Why is it there is such inordinate love for titles? Why does the barber who draws a tooth want to be called a doctor in a short time? or the ordinary dentist almost feels himself insulted if doctor was not prefaced to his name? The druggist, who probably cannot inform you how many per cent. of copper or iron there is in sulphate of iron and copper; or has acquired the knowledge to write their chemical formulas, wants the name of doctor applied also. The Captain of the chain-gang, after his office has expired, is a Captain still; the Judge forever remains a Judge, even if he only occupied the position in the lowest Court. The country is overstocked with Professors, Majors, Colonels and Generals, some of whom cannot lay the slightest claim to the titles applied. Then gentleman and lady are so frequently applied that it threatens to push the honest names of man and woman out of the way. A man may register his name at the hotel he stops at as John Brown and lady, but wife would be more honest, for the lady is often a little doubtful, while the true woman is not. I might enlarge upon the subject, but there are other matters to speak about

"Where then is all the boasted love of republicanism? Do not the signs of the time already point to a favored class who would like to rule over others?

"If there is no danger at present, the time will come when a man in possession of fifty to sixty millions of dollars will or may be looked upon with suspicion. The extremes may join hands, for a man possessing such wealth wields a mighty power if the times are favorable, and as most people of your country hold money in the highest estimation, and are under the impression that it causes the greatest imaginable happiness on earth, it would be strange if patriotism could not be sacrificed for money and promises in the distant future. There lurks, then, a greater danger than your foreign-born citizen."

"But, Mr. Lucifer, what can be done to prevent people from becoming wealthy? It is a right which every civilized nation allows its inhabitants for energy, brains, or foresight, and sometimes it is said good luck has something to do in the accumulation of wealth," I inquired. He answered:

GREAT WEALTH TO BENEFIT THE LOWER CLASSES.

"I would suggest not to hinder them, if it has become a passion with them like the gambler. Men who have accumulated in a short space of time, by speculation, forty millions to fifty millions of dollars are open to some eccentricities, to say the least. But they love the life they have become accustomed to, and have learned how to make ventures turn out profitable, while nine hundred and ninety-nine men do not or cannot, owing to the want of money and acquired knowledge. When a man is in possession of say from three millions to ten millions of dollars, his confidence in himself ought to be strong enough to keep himself out of the poor-house. He ought to be in a financial position to think himself enabled to live respectably. If he is not satisfied and desires more, let his income be taxed accordingly. The greater the wealth and income, the greater the taxes after the boundary line is reached. The man can therefore gratify his desires, but pays accordingly, and his wealth then is trimmed down to a normal state. Speculation now carried on in the world does not always create. Many men have become rich out of enterprises which had no money value at all, at the beginning nor end. Tell me where the benefit lies when the workers in your factories, of both sexes, invest in such enterprises? A thing that has no value and out of which no value can be worked, squeezed, pressed, or hammered by the aid of fire, water, and dynamite, cannot bring a profit in the end excepting to those who launch the fraudulent enterprise. If men can be permitted by a government to withdraw money in this manner, which is earned by the sweat of the brow or by industry, it is fair and just that a portion be returned to those whose failures, hopes and expectations they have wrought.

"I would take this money thus gained and use it for the benefit of the working class and the nation, but principally for educational purposes, and to a certain extent, charity too. Let your technical schools and similar institutions spring up all over the land, where your young of both sexes will learn how to earn a respectable living. Let the trades be taught, arts, cookery, lace-making, carving, and hundreds of similar occupations. Give free admission to all colors and religions, not even keeping your Indian from acquiring a little knowledge to preserve his race. A portion of this money could also be devoted to the advancement of the Indians. The Indians must be treated as children; they must be treated honestly and be taught to make themselves self-sustaining, otherwise it might be more charitable to fence them in and have your Gattling guns to play upon them, as the fireman does at a fire with his machine; one has a tendency to put out a fire and the other the lives, and that would be more charitable than to have them die by the aid of lightning whisky, starvation, and your free white American citizens of the 'Far West.' Those Indians who cannot be civilized must be made to understand that murdering any of their own race or the whites cannot be tolerated and must be punished by death. If they continue their warfare, as in some territories of the Pacific States, they must be treated as such human beings deserve, and this is death. It would, however, be a difficult matter to keep your average christian from a scalping tour about the time his mother, wife, and children have been murdered, and this has occurred not a few times, to the Indians, in the history of the American people who speak two separate languages. The relative of the Indian may be of no consequence, but he takes revenge, sacrificing life ten fold for the act inflicted upon him by the white race. Before judgment is passed upon another, reflect what you would have done if situated thus and thus, and always consider that your race is called civilized, and that you are noble Caucasians. But your noble Caucasian has quite a number of times acted no better than the savage, and not a few times acted as a leader in a great carnage. I must not, however, be carried away by the Indian question.

"With this money the unfortunates could be aided—the convict, the girl who has fallen, and the drunkard. Rewards could be given to worthy persons who have saved lives and property on water and land, frequently sacrificing their own lives, and taking away the support of a whole family, or of the young and aged.

"Almost every country has shown some favor to those who have saved lives—some reward, some medal, or recognition by the government has been given—but with you the whole is left to private parties. Only of late has some attempt been made to reward such people, but it is not sufficient. The man who, at the risk of his own life, saves a railroad train, with all its living freight, from destruction, is certainly worthy to be recognized, not only by the company who employs him, but also by the Government of the United States. Such recognition need not necessarily be very expensive, but when life is sacrificed in the attempt to save other lives, both the company and the government ought to show some recognition to the living, if in poverty; or to a wife and children, or such relatives as depend upon him for support.

"These are only a few of the benefits to which this money could be applied, but the uses would be many for such purposes.

"The money should never be used for the purpose of paying off the debts of the government, a State, or for any political or religious purposes of any party or sect. There must be no distinction between white and black, Jew or Christian, Democrat or Republican, rich or poor, foreign born or native; the benefits should be meted out alike, and I assure you the income to the nation would more than balance the outlay of the rich man, who can well afford to part with it without any injury to himself.

Thousands of young men and women would thus be brought up to some industry which would enable them to make a living, and thereby be kept from doing harm to themselves and others. Idlers must live, as well as those employed, but having no occupation, they are compelled to choose dishonest pursuits, which eventually will place them somewhere to be put under lock and key, and in this, as in nearly all cases, it signifies increase of taxation, or support, by the producing classes.

STRIKES.

"I am aware that the doctrine is called socialistic, but you will remember my idea is that both the rich and poor wield too great a power, which must be pruned down if you want to keep the tree of State in proper shape. There is, indeed, a great deal which requires regulation; for instance, spasmodical disturbances and strikes have a tendency to cause great losses. It causes uncertainty, loss of confidence, and places those who rely upon their wages from week to week, in a worse condition, by the stoppage of work. The poor man cannot remain idle long, with his family depending upon his labor, while the capitalist, despite the losses he sustains, need not personally suffer.

"Should a strike be entertained, there ought to be previous negotiations, and workmen employed on public highways ought not to be permitted to strike unless giving one or two weeks' notice. In the meantime the whole trouble might be amicably settled by arbitration of trusted and honest men of both sides.

"If men who are employed by railroads to move trains, or by a regular line of steamers, or gas and water works, and similar public institutions necessary to a whole city or community, are permitted, without notice, to go on a strike for higher wages at any moment, it may be the cause of more extensive outbreaks. Working people do not, in all cases, fully investigate, but rely upon others to do their thinking, and those who think for them are often found impracticable by entertaining socialistic views; or even worse, are dishonest, or have little revenges to carry out concerning themselves and employers alone.

"Sometimes these strikes are organized when there is not the slightest hope of success, simply because there is no urgent demand for the laborer, who can easily be substituted by another only too glad to take his place. The profits, too, sometimes are so small that the manufacturer makes barely both ends meet, or is storing up goods for better times. Then some would-be smart man, who desires to swing himself into a political position, causes his comrades to be dissatisfied, and they strike. They strike, of course, in the wrong time, and must become the main sufferers. There is a law which controls this, as well as other things. When there is a demand for laborers, then everywhere extra labor is demanded; but when work is not in demand, discharges are made, and if some fools then organize a strike, then you may look to see not a few financially used up, as is always the case. The consequence is, instead of these people causing times to improve, they only make everything about them appear more discouraging and unhappy.

"You must have laws to regulate these periodical disturbances, frequently causing great loss, in a commercial point of view, as well as the loss sustained by the contracting parties (employer and employee), besides the inconvenience it causes, and not unfrequently crimes, too, are committed; therefore the government and every State ought to make efforts to have laws enacted having a tendency to protect not only the workingman, but the employer, too, who is generally made responsible to the public in not fulfilling contracts entered into.

TREATMENT OF INEBRIATES.

"On the temperance question I have already given my opinion, viz: that drunkards be confined in asylums erected to cure this vice or infirmity. The money used for this purpose, if not taken from the State's resources. should be apportioned from the surplus income of the wealthy by the government, as in such undertakings every State must keep step with the advancement made. If this is not practicable, it is still cheaper for the State to take care of your drunkards, and the necessary funds must be applied, as for the insane. Opium eaters must share the same fate.

"Previous to this, enforce your laws already made; tax those who sell intoxicating liquors higher; make them responsible when they sell to a known drunkard, or to a child, in the same manner as you do when liquors are sold to Indians.

"The boys, in general, enjoy too much liberty in places where alcoholic drinks are sold, and those who violate the laws by selling liquors to boys under age, and are convicted several times, ought to have their licenses taken away forever in that State.

EFFECTS OF TREATING.

"Another great assistant to your drunkenness is the so-called 'treating,' or of one man paying the whole bill. This custom is to a certain extent also carried on in England, but in no country is it carried on so extensively as it is in the United States, and particularly in the West. The foreigners of all classes have a sort of instinct for it, as a duckling that naturally is attracted to the water, despite all the coaxing of the foster-mother hen to keep it on terra firma. So on the arrival of these foreigners, it requires little or no instruction to make them understad 'boys, take a drink.' The custom is irrational, causing men to drink frequently a great deal more than intended, and then by all that is not always a financial benefit to the dispenser of the liquids. If five men meet at a bar and take five drinks, each showing or wanting to show his liberality, or pay back the debt of hospitality so to say, there might be no danger, or if the whole number were used to take five drinks in short succession without even sitting down. But several may already feel the effects of the second or third drink, and by the time the fifth round is set up by the artist behind the bar, they are so jolly that they feel like treating all around several times in succession, spending often money that should go to the family not in over-easy circumstances, but now expended only to cause injury to the dispenser and the four companions too. If treating had not been resorted to, some of these men would have taken, in the time they had been joined, say sitting down leisurely, from two to five glasses, according to their habits and constitutions. All would have met their wives and children in a sober condition, while by the practice of this pernicious treating custom they return without money and very little brains not in possession of King Alcohol It will be very difficult to break up this much spread custom which, on closer investigation, has caused incalculable injury. No laws can be enacted, as it is a voluntary affair, but if the habit could be broken up many families in the future would be spared misery and want. There is more in such habits than some people imagine. Beyond the sea, in France, Germany, Austria, and other countries, this custom has no foothold. The gentleman or gentlemen you are engaged in conversation with, sitting at some table, would not feel themselves flattered if you wanted to show your liberal American qualities by paying for the company for one round, rushing down the liquids in opposition to their inclinations, and then expecting for the next to pay. The whole thing might be looked upon as an insult, and is not expected or wanted, and besides there are financial reasons also with not a few.

"There are several reasons why Europeans, particularly the Germans, who drink mostly beer, are not often seen inebriated in their own country, and they are: Strong alcoholic beverages are very seldom used, and only in minute quantities as appetizers. Wine, but mostly beer, is drank, and in all those places the opposite sex— the wife, mother, sister, and sweetheart—are not banished, but have free access with their male companions. It is obvious wherever your mother, wife, and sister can be taken, it is supposed that the male species will show some respect to the sex, as well as themselves too. Then a reasonable time is given for each to drink, depending on appetite and condition of the purse; and besides in all these places eating as well as drinking is indulged in, and other beverages can be partaken of, as tea, coffee, chocolate, etc. These are causes studied by us tolerably well during our periodical visits over your little world," said Lucifer, "and if they could be introduced to your nation the benefits would be manifested soon.

There has been considerable written and talked about this temperance question, but thus far your people still consume so many million gallons of alcoholic and strong liquors, some of it so strong too that it kills many in the outskirts of civilization, and it makes too, annually, many docile Indians, who were sent to their happy hunting grounds a little before their time. But all the fanaticism has not helped the matter much, or no more than a human being is prevented if he or she is intending to commit suicide. If poison is used, the person is aware it kills, so if the razor is sharp it will cut the throat, the dagger well pointed and guided will enter the heart, and so many glasses strong liquor not needed will make drunk, and frequent indulgences of that sort will cause death or worse than insanity. All this is well known previously, but God gave you reason to use all these things for some purpose, but it must be judiciously and moderately applied. So many glasses good wine will make your heart glad and have it forget the cares of life, and so many more glasses will make a fool of you by making your bed under the table. Your reason ought to be in a condition to judge the best, but if you persist in making a fool of yourself you must be put where no wine is to be had, and the strong arm of the law ought to do its duty. The causes and remedies have been pointed out, but the total abstaining from spirituous liquors will not be carried out for some time to come. Take the temperate view of it—learn to control yourself or abstain from it if preferable, but don't try to exercise a right to prevent others who are sober from using that which they have learned to use in a proper way.

"I am quite aware of the great injury the habit of using strong drink has caused, and few countries have suffered more than the United States of North America, but the remedy lies in their hands. 'The-must-not-and-shall-not-drink-policy,' in a Republic like yours, will never accomplish its end. Reason must dictate to every individual, and where it does not, confine diseased reason and individual too, until the intellect is restored, or has been taught the virtue of sobriety.

About this time I was somewhat annoyed, owing to the continuous attacks on the American people, and incidentally yawned. Thinking some remarks of politeness were necessary for this breach of good breeding, I remarked, "how quiet it is here."

He answered: "It is less quiet than you imagine. Could your semi-human senses, particularly sight and hearing, be advanced to the beings that surround us, you would wonder, and be delighted to the highest degree at what your eyes would behold."

"Could you not, by the aid of your power, render my senses more sensitive, in order to gratify me?" I asked.

"I admit," he answered, "to possees that power, but dare not violate the laws and rules without permission from higher quarters."

"Then please, worthy Mr. Lucifer, gain me, through your great influsnce that permission," I further begged. He stood reflecting, then as if communicating with some one, although no being was visible, and finally said:

A VISION OF HIGHER SPIRITS.

"Your request has been granted, but it is owing to your not belonging here yet, and of probably causing some good below. If you really were an occupant of the classes you have thus far seen, it could not be carried out. Every soul of a human being who enjoys what the higher elevated souls enjoy that surround us, must have attained the privilege, been educated or advanced to the standard they are entitled to, and when they have by their energy acquired the right, they appear as beings of higher spheres, with all the accompanying qualifications. The latter may be judged from your world below. For instance, a perfectly ignorant person who could neither read nor write, and did not enjoy a civilized life, may generally be picked from a number of smart lawyers, intelligent doctors and university professors. It would be strange indeed if his intellectual physiognomy would eclipse the others in apparent wisdom. Now what is it but the soul, through knowledge, that shines forth? After the soul has advanced thus far it may be left, so to say, like the infant when strong enough to walk alone, although it yet wants to be guided occasionally when traversing difficult and dangerous places. It may be compared to your scientific student, who has acquired requisite knowledge in the use of the microscope, telescope and spectroscope, or similar instrument. If he has acquired the necessary knowledge in the use of the instruments, he can act independent of the teacher, or exercise self-judgment. Let the uninformed or ignorant look through these instruments and their eyes will be wanting in the observations; i. e., many things will not be observed at all, and yet their sight may surpass that of the student. If, then, the soul is as far advanced, its faculties are armed—can penetrate. It knows why this and that is thus and thus on the world below, and here also.

"God everywhere has placed barriers which cannot be overstepped. Sometimes, but very seldom, visions are obtained; or instances occur where the soul of man appears to have exercised more than what is on an average allowed to man. He meant you simply to occupy the sphere assigned to human beings. The greatest or most famous astronomer is but little removed from the lowest type of a savage when it concerns the knowledge that concerns the soul alone; and thus it shall ever be, although upon all physical science you will continue to advance as heretofore, and more rapidly still. It is similar to the animals. You train dogs, horses, elephants, birds, and other animals, down to insects, to perform acts like human beings. Many of these animals have frequently become more gifted by the training than the same animals not trained, but the animal has not changed its shape or general character, but the horse, dog and elephant still represent those species. It has not learned to reason on the higher standard of the human being; and just so will your most learned philosopher represent but a man after all, and can only look into the mysteries he was desirous to fathom when the outer shell of man has been thrust aside as useless material that has served its time. But even after death the advancement is slow at first, because the soul still feels itself annexed to the body, and cannot at once throw off the influence the body had exercised over it during a lifetime. These are the great difficulties at the beginning. The habits or passions acquired cannot, at one sweep of the will, be eliminated, but as long as they remain they must necessarily retard the spirit's progress."

"Now you shall wonder, Mr. Smith," he said, as his tall, well-proportioned form, the figure of an Apollo, stood before me. He stretched out the fingers of both of his hands downward, so that the ends of the fingers gently touched my closed eyelids, and commanded me to look, saying, "Behold!" As rapid as the spark of electricity, or the flash of lightning, there appeared all around us on the enameled and beautifully ornamented floor, as well as under the immense crystallic roof of the place, beautiful human-shaped beings. They were mostly different from what I had previously seen. There appeared to be several gradations, but mostly of a higher order.

These spirits had the power, when they were hemmed in, to walk right through each other, without causing any change. This was apparent in the air, on the floor, and all around. The scene was like a vast aquarium peopled with beautiful spiritualized human beings. The five races of man, of both sexes, old and young, were represented, and generally there were small groups of the higher and lower orders found together in conversation, and upon all countenances, great celestial joy was visible, similar to a friend having found another friend, or relative, whom he had not met for many years.

During the time my sense of sight was feasting, the aural organs took in a sweet, murmuring, musical sound, emanating from thousands of beings. As all living creatures in great numbers will produce a characteristic sound, just so these beings caused a peculiar sound, which was most agreeable to the organs of my hearing.

When, at last, my astonishment and delight had partially been gratified, I made bold to ask Lucifer about the nature of this great meeting of so many souls, all feeling so joyful.

"These spirits," he began, "are mostly of a higher order than those you have thus far seen, but your sight has informed you of the gradation. The lower order are under our dominion, while those of a higher order are from beyond. In order to afford you a clearer insight into the method of entering on either side of this palace, I will explain to you the order of progression. In your world you were instructed, that when life's battle was ended, you would go to heaven, or hell. Some have a purgatory, too; and of late they have added a substitute for hell, which is termed hades. Call this a purgatory, if you choose; it is purging your souls, and preparing them for something better, as you have already learned; and you must admit that hoofed and horned devils, brimstone boiling, cauldrons of hot metal, hot pitch and oil, and all the tortures that a human being can be subjected to, as, for instance, by a holy inquisition, have not the remotest foundation, and would, if carried out, have not the slightest effect, as we have nothing to do with the grosser substance you left behind. We have to mold and put in order the crooked and deformed mind, or soul, and that is not material upon which heat has any effect.

"The whole thing is imaginary, and has no foundation whatever. You have been initiated sufficiently to be now better informed. At the beginning you have learned that but exceedingly few enter through the little gate or door where St. Peter presides as Grand Doorkeeper, and those who enter can only attain the second grade or circle, sphere or whatever you are pleased to term it. Not one in ten millions ever entered the third. But as the Deity designed that not a single soul is to be lost, they are passed over to us to prepare them for their advancement, and after they have passed the third degree, they are transferred to the more permanent part of the palace to begin their work for the higher attainments.

"From this you may judge that the teachings and the necessary progress made in the third heaven or hades are similar, and after the same has been acquired, all human passions of low order have been forever neutralized or eliminated. The third order is consequently a sort of stepping stone to the higher elevations, and from there to advance from glory to glory. Being made acquainted with the order of progression, your question will now be answered regarding the object of the meeting of the souls that surround us.

"The spirits, Mr. Smith, that appear to you more elevated or look more angelic, are from the other side. They are members of various degrees but none of very high order are present. The object of the meeting is to see friends and relatives from below, this being the first time the spirits on this side are permitted to see their relatives who preceded them. Those on this side must have attained the second degree before any permission is given to be present at a similar meeting. The visits cannot be returned, for no one can enter on the other side who has not attained all the perfections requisite, or the third degree. These meetings are of great benefit to those on this side. As you are aware now that a great deal depends upon the energy and will of the soul to advance here, it is obvious that their friends on the other side stimulate them to attain their perfections more rapidly, for then it will be far easier to meet more frequently on the other side. It is necessary, as previously stated, that all the grosser passions must be wiped out, and the nobler ones must be purified and brought up to the standard requisite here. Love, for instance, is not a passion intended to be obliterated, but it must be made pure and holy. There is nothing in the world below to draw any comparison, but the nearest is the pure love a mother entertains for her child. You may see such love in the five spirits approaching us. Those three beautiful beings of both sexes with the two less spiritualized shades, are parents and children. The father and mother died several years ago, the wife dying first and two months after, the husband. They are both in the second sphere at present, and the visit of the children is their first. The latter have died many years ago, but love holds its sway—it is carried beyond death and rises to the highest pinnacle, while hate could not be tolerated here. But both hate and love are deeply impressed upon the mind of man, and even the higher class of animals share in these passions on the world below, as you well know.

"The meeting is, as you perceive now, one of the periods—days you would call it below—when the higher classed spirits from the other side are permitted to visit their friends and relatives on this side, and that extends to the second and third circle. This assembly has only connection with the second degree; the third is more elevated and further in the interior. The periods assigned to this purpose are something similar to one of your holidays, but rather more with the holidays of the older country. Your Fourth of July as a holiday would be a poor comparison, and Christmas belongs more to the little ones. The fact is, you have not many holidays in your country yet—many people even begrudge Sunday rest. The lower order cannot take part in these exercises, but they are very well informed about it. Not a few are stimulated to attain this first privilege. All are anxious to come in contact with their departed friends known previous to their own demise on earth.

"A great deal more might be added in behalf of this assembly, but time is precious. I have still considerable to acquaint you with, and your body below is already mourned as dead. It behooves us therefore to leave these happy souls, and enter still deeper into this vast city under one roof. My intention is to give you our views before your return, in a straight forward manner, and it shall be regarding your nation, and you may, if you choose, set the conversation afloat, to bear fruit or good results. We will walk on until we arrive at the first small park, when we will continue our conversation.

From the circular large space where the spirits had congregated, there radiated in every direction of the compass avenues, streets or corridors, and we took one extending north, which simply meant to go deeper in the direction we had commenced. The roofs of the corridors were much higher, and more artistic architecture was displayed in the construction of the whole, when compared with the class shown in cells and rooms. The exterior throughout showed a higher tone, but the interior was not made visible to me, as probably the time was wanted for it. Only here and there were attendants visible, passing in and out from the apartments. They appeared of the higher order of beings, similar to my guide, and they may have been instructors or teachers. We finally arrived at the park, a magnificent garden of the most fragrant and gorgeous flowers, displayed in beds of the most beautiful design. Here and there large fountains played, forcing the liquid, clear as purest crystal, parallel to the tree tops some distance off. The trees further off were of immense hight, to which the California giants are but infants, and yet they were not so large in circumference, which caused them to look very graceful as they extended upwards straight as a molded candle. Others not so tall extended their limbs over a large space, the foliage almost touching the ground. Both trees and foliage of various varieties, some bearing beautiful fruit, others gorgeously colored blossoms, shedding their fragrance about like orange blossoms, looked different than any before seen in the world below. The limbs were alive with songsters, some of the most gaudy plumage. They surrounded us on all sides and appeared to address their songs and cries to my attendant, who, however, paid no apparent attention to them, or no more than any one who is familiar with an object or thing. Selecting seats under one of those curious patriarchs which sent out its corkscrew-like, twisted limbs, around which the graceful twigs and leaves were falling, he began:

"I have something to communicate to you, as already stated, and it consists of various matters to which immediate attention should be paid by your nation. Some of the questions are of the highest importance, and the time has arrived when a change becomes a matter of necessity, if future generations are not to suffer by it."

With this preface Lucifer continued, saying:

"You must admit, Mr. Smith, comparatively speaking, your nation is very young—one short century—but during this short period it has made giant strides in civilization, by which nations are judged. Your steam engines on water and land have caused revolutions in labor. Your telegraphs give facilities to communicate thoughts to distant points in a few minutes, where it formerly required five or six months. All the new discoveries of late have a tendency to shorten labor. A great deal of this progress is attributed to the form of government, and still more the superior intelligence of the people. Very seldom is any credit given to the immense resources you have in your country from which you can draw your supplies and riches. To acquire the latter or concentrate it, the methods adopted are not commendable. Frequently the destruction caused in the future, to coming generations, is far greater than the gain to one or a few. But we will come to that in our conversation.

"Your nation may be compared to a young giant—he has youth and strength, but lacks the experience of his father, consequently if not guided, or he will not heed advice, he will fall into the samo errors which his father was compelled to correct, but it was done by suffering losses, which is the general task-master of man. Europe represents the father, Asia the grandfather; both have suffered and much vitality was sacrificed in days gone by. The same will happen to the young giant, if he continues iu the ruts in which his vehicle of civilization runs. The young generally deem themselves more intelligent than the parents, and there never was a time when this idea has reached a higher stage than at present, and particularly is this applicable to your people. And yet dearly purchased experience that guides you throngh life or assists in doing so, is not so easily gained. Book learning often points out to you the dangerous places, but they are seldom remembered. But let a man be wrecked on a dangerous rock, he will forever remember the locality, and if in the future he comes in close proximity, he will try to steer clear of the invisible rock. By the loss sustained then his memory has been sharpened. By not heeding the past or preparing from it future safeguards, comes the reason history repeats itself again and again—just the same as if on a great public highway there was a great hole slightly covered up. Those traversing over it would be engulfed if they did not heed the advice of those who described the dangerous locality to them. Your species has, by all the great boasting, advanced but little if any at all; in fact it would be most difficult to suppress what has been born with yon. Since you are human beings you must have passions, and these passions remain with you as long as life lasts. In this the savage, as well as the highly civilized people of the world, are almost the same. It is owing to this that you still continue to murder each other on the battle field, and the advance in physical science has given you powerful agents by which you can cause terrific destruction to life and property. Your instruments of precision also give facilities to cause great destruction in the shortest space of time.

"If one was to judge by this destructiveness you at present cause in one battle, you should be considered worse in morals than formerly; but this is not true, for while you have learned to destroy, still more to disable, not kill, one branch of science has kept step in relieving the unfortunate—the wounded. All the higher classed nations must treat their wounded and prisoners far differently than the did four hundred years ago if they want to retain the respect of the world, and those who have been wounded are by this more humane treatment and the great advance in surgery, placed in a condition to regain their strength or save their lives. As in the individual so in nations, bloodshed and destruction could be prevented if one or both of the parties were capable of listening to reason. Arbitration, in many cases, would settle many difficulties and be the cheapest in the end, but the world is not prepared for it yet. The man's heart is by no means pacified who has a case decided against him by arbitration, if he thinks himself right. If it had come to a contest of strength, he might have considered himself even fortunate yet, if his antagonist only left a little life in his mutilated body. It is force against force with you still.

"When speaking of the passions of the human being, both civilized and uncivilized, there must be mentioned one powerful and most influential passion to which your civilized man is addicted, and this is the great desire to possess wealth or riches. In no country are the wealthy so highly honored and respected as in your country, and often in the search for it the goose is killed that lays the golden egg. In other words, in order to accumulate great riches, greater sacrifices have to be made either against their fellow man, living at present, or to those coming in the future. We will commence with the tiller of the soil in the United States of North America. Does he not continually rob Nature of its supply, from year to year, and returns nothing to her? The husbandman puts into the soil a certain kind of seed, every year alike, and grumbles at harvest time that the crop becomes less and less. Nature is well balanced. In order that a plant should grow healthy and produce a bountiful supply, some of the salts must be returned to the soil which former plants, in the process of growing, withdrew. It is true, the carbon is drawn from the carbonic acid in the air, but that only. The consequence is, as already stated, the supply is exhausted, and if by that time your rancher, or farmer, is not sufficiently rich he will go with the family further on, away from built up settlements, and repeat the process on a larger scale, perhaps.

But there must be a stop to this sort of farming if the large immigration from Europe continues, and the natural growth of the country is not retarded by epidemics. All vacant space in your country will be taken up, and then you will be compelled to pursue the same course as the parents have on the other side of the big water. In your State both fruit and vegetable have grown much smaller, although the climate, to which you attributed the large size attained, is still the same. It is hardly twenty years passed over, and then not an insect molested your beautiful fruit, while now you may look with suspicion upon many luscious fruits into which some destructive insect has drilled a hole to lay its eggs. Why is this? Do you think there was not a remedy formerly to keep insect life down, or Nature's laws more in equilibrium? Much is said about the introduction of new species of destructive insects from the older States, but nothing is said of the human benefactors which the wanton destructiveness of men and boys cause when they are permitted to gratify their lust to kill. The boasted liberty in America, and shooting down whatever is' liked, has already shown itself in the depopulation of the feathered tribe and useful animals. It is true you have laws which should protect some useful birds and game, but as such law-breakers are seldom punished the same violence is continued. In shooting down your insect-eating birds you increase the insects; the insects destroy your fruit and thereby repay you for the sin committed.

"A great deal of the happiness of the human race depends upon the lower animals, but how ruthlessly they are often treated. Some of those useful birds that consume in their breeding season, for themselves and families, from four thousand to five thousand insects and eggs per day, have been permitted to be destroyed.

"Frequently the orchardist, owing to the attack on fruit, destroys birds also, although they may have earned more than their 'bread and butter' previously in saving his fruit.

"It must be remembered that even grain, or seed-eating birds, are, by nature, compelled to apply insect food to the young baby bird, and, consequently, much insect food must be consumed. The young animal, in the application of its food, is similar to the human being, or higher animals, which require the mother's milk first, until sufficiently advanced to live upon grosser food. The baby bird requires insects first, and the parents must furnish the supply as a necessity.

"This wanton destruction of the feathered tribe has been the cause, partially, of getting nature out of equilibrium, and man is here directly to blame. Why should he not suffer for the result? The despised animal known as the bat, is often used in trap-shooting in your State, and is then sacrificed to your moloch called 'sport,' to be shot or maimed; and yet these animals, in order to sustain their life, consume food which is troublesome to man as insects. Where does the bat do harm otherwise, that they should be sacrificed thus? Even an ugly amphibious animal, like the toad, is laboring for the benefit of man when placed in his garden. The ant, also, is a great destroyer of insects which cause injury to man indirectly. The Ruler has arranged nature thus, that one must live upon the other; if, therefore, you destroy those who assist you, it will follow that you are made to suffer yourself.

"When grasshoppers and crickets overwhelm you, you resort to prayer, and God-deliver-me-from-evil policy, and yet it would be as much of a miracle to stop those creatures, as it would be to prevent water from running down the hill by praying against it.

"In the older countries the greatest attention is paid to the birds, and boys are not permitted to molest them, or treat them unkindly, by throwing stones at them, or by destroying their nests; and in the winter, when the ground is covered with snow, they are frequently fed by the governments and kind persons, well knowing that it will be returned in many ways.

"A true Christian does not only display his charity to his own species, but he must also include the animal. The Hebrew and heathen, or the humanitarian, may outrank him, and in this some of the older nations preceding the Christians have shown far more charity than your pretended followers of Christ. The Newfoundland dog who has saved his master, and several of his children subsequently, from drowning, ought certainly deserve to be fed until his life's battles with other dogs are ended, but how often is he? The horse who on the race-track caused his master to win thousands of dollars, has to die an ignoble death; or if, by his great fleetness, he has saved his master's life on the battle-field—does he often draw any benefit from it? Very seldom is a man found who keeps such a horse the balance of his life.

"The Supreme Being gave man the power to rule the earth, and if well done, he will reap the benefit. In every well regulated country it is in his power to diminish all vicious and destructive wild animals if they are dangerous to the life of man, or his property. On the other hand, it is in his power to increase his flocks—cattle, sheep, goats, horses—and he knows he is the gainer thereby; but his ignorance may be so great that he destroys animals who may be his best friends, although he does not draw a direct benefit as he does from the animals mentioned; but they keep insect life down, preventing them from feeding upon the products of man, and such animals are the birds. There is such a thing as 'sport,' and the huntsman may take animal life, but when he sacrifices, when he kills the mother that bears the young, all honest sport ceases. When the fisherman visits one of your lakes to amuse himself during his leisure hours in angling, he may find pleasure in hooking fish, but if the same man is not satisfied, and resorts to foul means, using powerful explosives, killing young and old by the thousand, and depopulating a whole lake of its finny tribe, there cannot be any sport or pleasure, but only criminality, which ought to be, all over the land, most severely punished. This applies equally to all game shot out of season, and certain birds at any time. In allowing these people to continue in their destructiveness to animals, you allow them to kill the goose that lays the golden egg.

"If it were not for a few wise men in your nation who have become deeply interested in fish culture, many of the rivers would now be but poorly supplied with fish, and those which have gained a supply the vandals are already working, on a wholesale system, to gain the dollars. All this you have got to change if you desire to protect the coming generations. The laws already made, covering these cases, ought to be executed, and if not stringent enough, made so by enacting other laws to cover the cases. But the main thing is to punish."

REASONING POWER OF ANIMALS.

"It may not be amiss to say a few words more in behalf of the animals," said Lucifer. "The dumb brute is generally looked upon as possessing far less intelligence than it really does, and the less intelligence or education the judge, or human being, possesses himself, the less he will acknowledge to the animal. And yet, in very many cases, the instinct of the animal surpasses the wisdom or knowledge of the human being. The term instinct is usually applied to the animal, the average human being taking it for granted that the term applied is the proper expression. Your investigators, however, find that it is often difficult to say where instinct ends and reason begins. It cannot be termed instinct alone when an animal thinks and considers what to do next, and then carries its determination into execution. When the elephant goes into a jungle, and there breaks off a suitable stick by the aid of his trunk, and trims it to suit its purposes, and then deliberately uses the stick as an instrument to remove a parasite with which it is infested, removing it from a place which can only be reached by the aid of the stick, it exhibits more than instinct. Such an animal must reflect and think before it carries out its work. When the ant, a small insect, finds food at a certain locality close to its nest, and the quantity is too large, it leaves it, and returns with comrades to remove it to the place. There is united thought and action, and time does not obliterate the thought, nor does the insect forget to return. Only when the deed is executed is it satisfied.

"Thousands of instances could I give to mankind of various animals who thus display more than instinct. It is reasoning, as in man, but less developed, and this would indicate something higher —would here also point to something more elevated, which might be interpreted by not a few human beings as a soul, or an essence which controls the material of which the creature is made up, and that has resemblance to man. I will not, and dare not go too far in this direction. Suffice it to say that the vanity you entertain that everything upon your earth was created for YOUR special purpose is somewhat fallible. One thing is positive—every animal, every plant, every mineral, has some function, some office to perform, although it may for the time not be known. The time may come, and in some instances it has come, when your science has penetrated the supposed mystery. And thus a horrible looking monster may prove itself a benefactor to man instead of being a dreaded enemy. The animals are far more related to you than you imagine, but as previously hinted, I dare not go farther in this direction. I will add in behalf of the brute creation, that the human being who shows no feeling for his dog, horse, or the animals under his control, can never be a good man or woman, be their profession to any religion followed as it will. Such a person lacks feeling to his fellow creatures and cannot be trusted with the control of men. Such men will always prove tyrants, and that mostly signifies cowards also.

"There are human beings now, and there have been in the older or Eastern countries thousands of years ago, who have allotted to the animals a soul, and a progressive one too.

"Have you never noticed, Mr. Smith, the resemblance of human beings to some species of animals, or have you never observed their actions showing similarity? The fox shows its cunning by the shape of its head and face. Are not the same features stamped upon the forms of human beings? Another shows stubbornness, still another courage or cowardism. Is not the same visible in many human beings? Compare the genuine bull dog with his big neck, to the wind-hound, the spaniel, and the lap-dog. You have all these human species amongst you. Many a man has a striking appearance to a bull dog, and when you meet such you instinctively give him a little more room than the spaniel looking genus homo, and you know full well why you do it too.

"Thus the outward structure and behavior of the man will give you an idea of his disposition and inclinations, and in but a few cases it requires the faculty of a La Vater to inform yourself pretty certainly that before you stands such and such inclined human being, if not animal. If, then, Darwinianism is admitted, physically speaking, why may you not go a step higher and admit the possibility of a further and higher progression likewise? But I am cautioned to rest upon this point, right here.

FORESTRY.

"In forestry, also, it is high time your State and the general government pay some attention. In the destruction of your forests you have no rival in the world. Some of the future aristocracy, those who intend to rule your country by their accumulated wealth, are doing their work now to cheat coming generations out of their birthright. What will be the effect eventually, say in a State like California, if the trees in the higher elevations are sacrificed? The great storage of snow piled up during winter in the higher elevation of your snow mountains, will have no protection when the sun will show its great power. The snow will melt long before its time, and the accumulated water will come booming down the valleys, overflowing your shallow rivers and causing death and destruction everywhere, where man had not securely fortified himself against it. After the snow is melted, when you had your abundance of water then comes the drought. But this is not all. It has been noted in other countries that wherever the forests were cut down entirely, great climatic changes took place which had a tendency to make a desert of the locality. Asia, in that respect, your grandfather, has suffered much in that direction. The land where once milk and honey flowed, was sacrificed by destroyers such as you have now in the upper regions of the Sierra Nevadas. But the older ones made slower work, for they had not fire and water harnessed up to do their work on a large scale, as numerous sawmills are doing now. They had to rely entirely upon the direct force of man or his muscles, and the work was necessarily slower on that account.

"Some time ago," Lucifer continued, "I made myself acquainted with a much lauded enterprise about to be carried out in your State. The enterprising genius is apparently one who intends to kill the goose that lays the golden eggs. As in all such undertakings, the man appears as a benefactor to the community. In this case the manipulator and would-be benefactor somehow comes in possession of a beautiful mountain lake, surrounded with fine timber. The idea strikes him that the timber at another locality, cut up in boards to build houses, which are easily burnt down, so in a short time a pretty large town can be wiped out—under favorable circumstances, in a few hours.' Well, at another locality these fine trees would be a fortune in the man's pocket. The difficulty is how to transport this valuable timber to the place, to saw it into boards. His genius for benevolence steps in and whispers to him, like a little bird from the tree tops, 'Tap the lake by a subterraneous channel, get up a grand irrigation scheme to benefit a million of people, more or less (on paper prospectus), and then you may easily cut down at your leisure all those fine, stately trees, at which old Mother Nature labored industriously for two or three centuries or more. After you get the money secure in a safe corner to make you a representative of a 'self-made man,' it is not absolutely necessary that the irrigation enterprise be carried out to the letter. Circumstances alter cases you know.'

"Should this one penny to the public and ninety-nine pennies into my own pocket individual, be enabled to carry out his great irrigation scheme, how long would the water run through the intended passage after the trees have been cut down that protected the water from rapid evaporation? Unless Nature has commenced to do her work differently, it would be miraculous that this man could fully carry out his enterprise, to be beneficial to others besides himself. Irrigation enterprises should be encouraged, as they will become necessary in the future, as you are gradually cultivating the soil to the various purposes to which the climate is adapted, but if a lake, a constant storage of water in the higher elevations of your mountains, a thing of beauty for all time to come, has to be destroyed in order to gratify the cupidity of one of your future money kings, then the government must be extremely weak or wicked, when it pretends to be so near sighted not to see such gross mistakes, such killing off of the geese that laid some of the golden eggs.

DESTRUCTION OF TREES ABOUT LAKE TAHOE.

"The interest in the affairs of the forest has been sufficient to induce me to make personal observations in one reported locality, some six thousand five hundred feet above the level of the ocean. A beautiful sheet of water, hemmed in by high mountains, and about twenty-two miles long to fourteen or fifteen miles wide, known as Lake Tahoe (formerly Lake Bigler), one of the largest mountain lakes in the world, whose scenery cannot be surpassed in beauty, must gradually suffer from consequences which are intended for the small lake previously mentioned.

"The outlet of this lake is known as Truckee river, passing through mountains, through which the constant force of water during ages has cut its channel, and which was and is almost solid rock. On either side of the river, up to the highest points, the trees have and are being cut down, leaving nothing but the waste and rocks by which they were surrounded and from which they grew. The logs are forced by devices direct into the low river to be floated to assigned places for cutting up at saw mills, and the refuse of the mills, as sawdust, is all passed into the river to pollute it. From the town of Truckee to the lake, some fifteen miles by stage route, on either side of the river, the trees are thus disposed of, in some localities not a tree remaining, and in less than three years the locality will be entirely cleared away. These trees have nearly all their roots imbedded in the cavities of the rocks, and in fact spring or grow right out of the fractured rocks. It may puzzle some of your species how these trees can exist, but it must be obvious to most of them that it required centuries in their naturally slow growth to have acquired the size which they had attained when cut down. If they are of the proper size, all are sacrificed and the barren rocks, decaying branches, or the charred remains of trunks and branches stare one in the face, representing a perfect chaos of disorder.

"When your investigation extends about the lake, you find your 'lumber fiend' was and is just as busy tumbling logs into the lake to be floated away. The size there is much larger, consequently the harvest much richer for fire and the human destroyer of forestry. In some localities the soil has been shorn of its forest giants, and ages will only give the same inviting aspect to the locality again, were the same kind of trees to grow, but instead of them only low and close shrubbery is replaced by Nature.

"The supply of water of the lake comes from the surrounding highly elevated mountains, covered with snow a large part of the year, and from natural springs in the lake or the mountain side, where the fluid of the upper regions is stored up in the bowels of the mountains nearer the lake and at a lower level.

"The observation was made that wherever there was a deficiency of trees caused either by the removal of the same by man or other causes prior to the arrival of your so-called civilized man, there Nature had no cause to send its supply of the fluid which makes the lakes. In other words, no springs issued from such localities at the latter part of August, 1882, when the visit was made. If any water issued from its source of storage it was lost by evaporation or found its way back to the rocky soil before any could reach the lake. The result must be apparent, if no provision is made to stop these ravages.

"Ages past this lake was much larger and deeper, of which you may find traces at different localities, one of the plainest being near 'Idlewild,' the summer residence of a rich lady from the Capital of your State. The wild-looking cliff in the rear is bound together cement-like, holding large boulders, pebbles, and gravel, all rounded off by the action of water or the force of wind and wave combined. This crag or cliff of conglomerate extends upward to a considerable hight, and if you take the trouble to climb on top, you will find other indications, one being several white sandstones weighing somewhat over a hundred pounds. They are foreigners there and only two forces have caused them to be at the described place, one being the action of a glacier and the other the receding of the water from the lake of which at one time the conglomerate formed the shore.

"To continue our conversation in behalf of the forest, it may be given out as a plea that the land has been legally purchased from the Government, and therefore the owner has a right to use his property as he chooses; but a government ought to be enabled to rectify its mistakes, particularly as in this case the land is not desired for agricultural purposes generally, as but little is fit for it, even when the trees are cut down. If, therefore, the surroundings have been denuded of its forest, it is robbed of all the value it ever possessed and will possess for centuries to come. You rob Nature in this case as you have in many other localities of much of her grandeur, and thereby not only impoverish your coming generations but at the same time lower the standard of intelligence of your nation before the advanced nations of Europe also. This applies not to a few localities in the United States.

"Some of the greatest sights, where the inmense forces of Nature exhibit themselves, are indifferently passed over, or are utilized to 'make money,' as the phrase goes. 'Make money,' that's the great lever, and the deity that appears to have infected the inside of temples as well as the gambling hell—all, all want to make money at once, it matters little what the future sacrifice turns out to be. Is this really true republicanism, or is it to build up better classes when you have them enriched sufficiently to rule over you?

"Returning to Lake Tahoe, I will add that just as the high mountains surrounding it are robbed of the trees, just so correspondingly will electricity occasionally show its terrific force in that vicinity in the future. The negative and positive electricity unite with the greatest violence imaginable, causing those terrible electric storms, when the waves run mountain high and appear to be drawn upward by some gigantic, invisible force. If the trees remain, the positive electricity above and about the lake will gradually and gently be attracted by the millions of points of the trees and branches, and they being connected with the earth, and consequently negative electricity, unite the two great forces at various points harmlessly, which would and could not take place with shrubbery, as it does not reach sufficiently high to meet the currents of positive electricity. If the trees are eventually removed, the future will show then when unification of electricity takes place; it will be on the principle of the 'Leyden Jar,' or 'Franklin's Panes,' with necessarily greater violence of course, sometimes causing loss of life and property.

"In this vicinity, too, Mr. Smith, it is probable you may look for the mysterious north wind, which, funnel-like, is supposed to swoop into your valleys, coming from some yet unknown locality. It is certain your men of knowledge say that it does not cross the Sierra Nevada mountains.

"I perceive you doubt the assertion, but on reflection may it not be possible when explained to you? Almost every human being of common intelligence will admit that there are certain attractive forces, or laws, that to a great extent govern your world in a physical sense. For instance, the living, as man, animal and plant, find their attraction in the opposite sex. The north pole of a magnet attracts the south pole of another magnet. The different gases have attraction for each other, or the gases unite with other elements, forming new combinations, and both static and galvanic electricity are attracted by their positive and negative forces towards each other. Science informs you that water, evaporating and condensing, produces, under favorable circumstances, electricity, and over a great lake like Tahoe it would be negative electric reaching to a considerable elevation. Admitting, then, that a strong current of air, or wind, at a still higher elevation, was passing over the lake, or its vicinity, could it not be possible that such a current of extremely dry air, which is highly charged with positive electricity, would be deflected from its course by the attraction in such close proximity, and in this case consisting of two attractive forces, negative electricity and air charged with moisture?

"Some scientists of your State have informed the world that the north wind is negative electric; if so, the earth itself must have become positive electric when a certain experiment is carried out at the time the north wind passes over the country for several days. The phenomena which manifests itself is this, and is carried out by means of an electrometer and a glass rod with rubber, upon which electric amalgam has been placed. If such a glass rod is excited by friction the gold leaf strips in the glass vessel diverge, being repelled from each other, owing to both being charged with positive electricity, and when the north wind blows, they remain extended for some time. Should the ball or knob above the glass vessel be touched, the leaves immediately collapse, because negative electricity from the earth was met and united. Such phenomena is, however, not always exhibited, as the experimenter may discover, for at times the leaves will not rush together when touched, but remain extended, as if still positive elecricity was offered, or added to it. What does this establish? Either that the earth or the person have become positive electric, or both.

"In order that deeper search may be made in this direction, this phenomena is only put forward as a hint, and it is well worthy further investigation. Owing to nature being partly out of equilibrium it is due that the north winds cause a sort of derangement with all living beings, and the lack of moisture in the air is not the only cause, as is often supposed.

USEFUL TREES.

"The wanton destruction of forests in the United States is forced to be a serious question in the future. In fact, in some of the older States the want of some kinds of the most useful wood in the arts and for manufacturing purposes, is already seriously felt. A wood-famine is bound to come, if no hindrance is to be placed in the way of those who have had the forests cut down. If the cutting of trees becomes absolutely necessary, the forests should not be entirely obliterated, but patches left here and there for the future. It is not, however, in the future use of the trees alone, but they have a function to carry out. They are placed there as sentinels, and to a certain extent control the climate. Some of your wise men who control printing presses, and send out their thoughts and opinions on paper daily, will have it that it makes but little difference about the trees being cut, as in a short space of time, nature shows herself in a different garb, forcing out shrubbery and thereby covering the naked soil more densely than before. True, very true, but what electric action would a low shrub perform so close to the soil? What conductors of electricity would they be when not in connection with the upper stratas of the air currents? I assure you, electricity plays a far more important part in meteorological phenomena, or the weather, than man of average intelligence supposes. Gradually it is dawning upon the world what a subtle, gentle, and at the same time all-powerful agent electricity is in its various application by man, or as static electricity by nature. But I must not be tempted into a scientific discussion on electricity. I am inculcating into your mind important matters on the wood question.

"I will continue. Such wood as the hickory and the black walnut have become scarce already—now, where is there such valuable wood obtained that supplants the elasticity and strength of the hickory? Fortunes could be made if some of the cultivators of the soil in your Western States had the foresight to leave patches of these valuable trees, but fire and the axe have done their work well and sure. Here is an item in one of your journals, going the rounds: 'Some of the finest walnut trees in the mountains of North Carolina have been sold at $40 each, just as they stand in the woods, the purchasers reserving the privilege of taking them away within a certain number of years.' Another item in the newspapers mentions a farmer in Missouri who set out a grove of walnut trees twenty years ago, on waste land. They were recently sold for $27,000. These trees are excellent shade trees besides, and could frequently be substituted for such purposes in place of trees of which the wood is of less value. To cut it short, I cannot impress upon your mind too strongly the urgency for the protection of your future timber supply. It is plain enough that want must come, as you continually cut down but never replant as they do in other countries, under the supervision of the government.

SCHOOL OF FORESTRY.

"A school of forestry, if there is none in your country, ought to be established. From these, men could be drawn to superintend future undertakings. The laws that exist for the protection of the forests ought to be scrupulously enforced, and if not sufficiently stringent or covering a case, new laws ought to be enacted to be more effective. The bill should make special provisions against forest fires. Gross carelessness by hunters, sometimes accidental by the concentration of the sun's rays on broken bottles. The older governments, particularly Germany, may already give hints what course to pursue, for there this matter has been controlled effectively for many centuries, and it is surprising when you travel through the country what numerous forests, in small patches, are found here and there, and the most are produced by systematic planting of the trees at certain localities adapted for the trees, or to aid as protection to the locality.

"During my discourse to you, I mentioned the effect the melting snow has upon the rivers and valleys below, if the trees are permitted to be cut down entirely. I am aware some good people in some towns of the Sacramento Valley, make known to the world that the so-called hydraulic system of mining has been the sole cause of inundations and destruction to property, but despite my sympathy being for the husbandman and those who cause permanent settlements, I yet insist and adhere to my views, that the wholesale cutting down of the forest trees has been and will be an important factor, to make you feel, to say the least, very uneasy sometimes in your valleys in the future."

HYDRAULIC MINING.

At this I suggested that he give his views upon hydraulic mining, as the country was deeply interested in that question at present. He began thus:

"Every well regulated government is compelled, in order to assist the country to protect its rivers and highways, and any country that ignores the tiller of the soil, allowing its land to be destroyed forever, and the families impoverished, must itself feel the effect in time, even if at another locality, a few men have enriched themselves, in being permitted to carry on their mischievous work. The genius that causes your Asiatics, under the guidance of a white man, to point his powerful monitors or water-giants upon the mountain side, causing to crumble before him the whole mountain, which he gradually washes into the rivers and valleys, and leaving the much coveted yellow metal in safe places to collect; this genius, and another who commands numerous white and yellow attendants armed with axes, high up in the mountains, causing the monarchs of the forest to fall before him—these two go hand in hand; one fills the rivers with mountains of debris, and the other genius or fiend causes the mighty currents of melting snow to sweep over the filled up rivers, inundating and destroying fertile valleys, farmhouses and towns, or all before them. Can you afford, can the government tolerate this sort of freedom forever, without being itself destroyed by it? Is it judicious, wise and justifiable for a government to allow a few to become wealthy at the expense of the many by destroying not only property that belongs to the nation, but cultivated, valuable real estate, for the future or several generations?

"The property of the agriculturist must forever be an inheritance to the coming generations. As long as he possesses his land it will be a constant and more trustworthy mine to work than any hydraulic mine. The products of the husbandman are necessary in all countries, while gold is not absolutely so. The idea I wish to convey is that you cannot subsist upon gold; that circumstances may cause a pound of food to be of more value than a pound of gold, because the first is necessary to sustain life, while any other purchasing power or medium may be made to represent gold.

"If you cover the land of your agriculturist with the material washed down by the aid of water, little giants and big giants, manipulated by the sons of the Flowery Kingdom, you destroy its productiveness almost forever, and that signifies the abandoning of the land and all the improvements—it means the driving out not only of one family but thousands, who would in future have cultivated the soil had it not been destroyed. Such perpetual mines of rich soil and favorable climate have in the older countries been worked thousands of years, and yet every year a new supply is furnished if the worker does his duty. The gold mine once worked out has all life worked out of it. The man who has filled his pockets from the product of the mine has no love for the locality out of which his riches have been taken that makes him feel as big and heavy as a toad loaded down with shot. Then where is the improvement that these classes cause to spring up about them? Is there any sign that shows any permanency, as in the farmer, who anchored himself to his possessions and around him spring up new cultivators, which eventually signifies new fields and orchards, more houses, then villages, stores, manufactories, school houses, churches, law and order, prosperity and contentedness of many people.

"The site may even be forgotten by that time, from which 'Self-Made Pomposity' got his wealth, had he not caused such great disturbance to the ground with his little rock and debris lifters, named Monitor and Little Giant.

"Agriculture, therefore, from this or on the threatened land represents a constant income in the future, which tends to build up a community, building villages and towns, bringing peace, plenteousness and happiness, generation after generation, while the destroyer of the land may live in plenty in a foreign country, or packed his wealth amongst the future nabobs of a large city. From the past judge the future. Where are your rich mining towns and their improvements termed permanent? The wealth has been scattered all over the world.

"It is necessary sometimes, in order to judge the real value of a thing, not only to consider the present but the future also; now, it is a well known fact that the cities in all civilized countries are steadily and surely increasing in population, in the older countries even by the tide of immigration that annually finds its way in ships to your shores, these cities still increase. If the population of cities is to live upon food, the work of producing it depends upon the cultivator of the soil, and that means the larger the people are represented in the cities, just so in ratio must the acreage be increased or new soil broken.

"Now your great Sacramento valley alone, when put in a proper condition by the aid of both Government and State, can be made to yield food to feed at least ten millions of people. Of course, it requires a great outlay of money to make some of the richest land productive and secure, which is partially, or yet under water. If the redeeming of this land is left to private enterprises, it will require many years yet to cause the same to be useful. There must be a united and simultaneous movement by the Government to aid in the improvement and protection of the land. It would, indeed, be humiliating, if the valley is left to be destroyed, when it offers so much in the future. It is really killing a pretty big goose that lays large-sized golden eggs.

"As one who is supposed to know your species pretty well, having had under my care so many characters, I may add my idea, and it is this: The gold in your mountains is an established fact, and just so long as the much-coveted yellow metal lies there undisturbed, just so long will the cupidity and general love for gold by man strive to extract it. If your laws are wise, preventing the heretofore adopted system of extracting the gold, and filling rivers and valleys below, it will by no means stop the work to procure the gold by some other means, and if injury is not caused, will, of course, be permitted to be carried out. Sooner or later the tempting metal must come out, or my faith in the Yankee spirit has not been well placed. In many localities the cultivators of the soil, in which the orchardists and similar occupations are included, and the miner, must go hand in hand, often representing one and the same person. The man may milk his mine, as he does his cow, and for this there is a proper time, or when not occupied in his other industries.

"The surface belongs to the tiller of the soil and his associates; the bowels of the earth to the miner; and there are countries where both are well worked, the tiller of the ground using his plow and spade in closest proximity to the dumps of the quartz mines."

THE WATER USED FOR IRRIGATION.

"As in other countries, so it will be found in your State, that the land is of great value, despite the fact of its being more elevated. You have, besides, the great advantages in climate, for wherever the fluid can be placed that the hungry and thirsty plant requires for its nourishment, there it will flourish and thrive. If the law of the land compels those who have invested large capital in hydraulic works to discontinue the methods they have adopted to extract the gold from the mountains, they must utilize the force of water for more peaceful purposes, i. e., making their outlay remunerative by selling the water to the tiller of the soil for irrigation purposes, and by this method the loss sustained, to a certain extent, may be of the greatest benefit to many people. In carrying out such plans it will, however, be necessary for the capitalist, as well as for the State itself, to show greater energy in bringing to your mountains the requisite and proper immigration from the various countries of Europe, or those best adapted for the cultivation of the particular plant, or plants, to which the soil and locality has been specially found to be adapted, and to most localities, not too greatly elevated, the grape-vine and the numerous fruit trees have already proved themselves to be profitable in their cultivation. Thus it may be found in twenty to thirty years the hydraulic works have shown themselves of great benefit—been, in fact, a sort of advance to a higher stage of civilization.

"Often what man considers a great injury, turns out in the end a blessing and benefit. It is reported that the time has almost arrived when the majority of your people residing in the Southern States will admit that the abolishment of slavery was a great benefit, rather than an injury, to a large community, despite the great financial losses connected with it. The time may also arrive when the same may be said regarding the hydraulic works of California. Gold was the first attraction that brought civilized man to your State, but the product gathered has been scattered over the world. Agriculture, and related sisters, have gradually supplanted the first industry, and are developing the whole State, and will hold the same in future, too; but the gold in the mountains still remains as a great treasure-house for coming generations, proving itself, when brought into concentration, a blessing or a curse, according to its application.

"There are people in your State so unreasonable as to say that it would have been far better for your country, and mankind generally, if the gold discoveries had never been made on your coast about the year eighteen hundred and forty-nine. In opposition to this, one might inquire what other attraction was there then offered to cause people to visit a comparatively unknown country? Believe me, Mr. Smith, as in nature, so in the history of man—there is a guiding force, which emanates from the highest fountain head, or the Ruler of the universe, and He that rules the universe not only designed to cause a great rush to California from all parts of the civilized world, in order to carry off the precious metals stored in the bowels of its mountains, but he intended, likewise, that the land should be peopled, and many happy homes established, by the industry of private individuals, and capitalists too. This theory will, of course, show my optimism; but my age, the preceding history of your world, and the great confidence I have in the wisdom of an Almighty Ruler, all point to the verification of the idea.

"Every great event taking place is therefore put forward as a forerunner that will cause some great revolution or change. Upon the same reasoning you may take for granted that an Alexander, Julius Cæsar, Napoleon, and other noted warriors, did not arrive without a design. Apply this to noted reformers, scientists, discoverers, music, art, and to general progression. Just when the proper time arrives, the tool or instrument to produce certain acts will be found ready; but as in the cultivation of a plant, it often requires previous preparation, and the proper time for the plant to take root and grow. I hope you will comprehend the philosophy, Mr. Smith, presented to you."

SECURIITY OF DAMS.

"But to return to hydraulic mining. Do you not think by impounding the debris from the mines by means of strong dams, the system adopted thus far could be harmlessly continued?" I asked.

Lucifer answered: "To a certain extent, yes; by building your dams secure and a number in succession equally strong, a great deal causing damage could be obviated. One strong dam still allows the suspended material to find its way into the rivers, and when the water is high the danger that these dams may cause is great. There are further, everywhere, unprincipled people who care not for life or property. The great forces which man now wields can be made use of. The force which causes the walls of fortifications to crumble to dust, or break tons of solid metal, could equally as well destroy your strongest dams. All the high explosives, or those which are converted from the solid to the gaseous state by heat and concussion instantly, are in a condition to be used by every ill disposed person. In spite of having laws enacted punishing the criminality to the greatest extent, you would have yet to catch your man before you hang him.

SACRAMENTO VALLEY—ITS FUTURE.

"Whether hydraulic mining be discontinued or not, whether dams be built or the water left to follow the laws of gravitation unhindered, it should not prevent the dwellers below from attending to the duty of fortifying its rivers and the towns against the periodical attacks of water coming down from such high elevations as your Sierra Nevadas. Every year a little ought to be added, and the older work faithfully inspected by competent persons. 'A stitch in time saves nine,' you know, and 'an ounce of prevention is better than a pound of cure.'

"This is one of nature's laws, the locality allows nature to carry it out, but the ingenuity of man, the mind, has control over matter and can hinder or lead nature's forces aside or away from the threatened place. It cannot be done in all cases, but this can be mastered. There is probably no country in your world, no matter how favored, which has not something that prevents it from being called perfect, according to man's theories. It is too hot, or cold; earthquakes shake it up too often; cyclones twist everything out of shape, whirling it into its whirlwind; hurricanes dash over the country, showing no more respect to the mansion of the rich than it does for the most insignificant hovel of the poor. On water and land, in the valley and high mountain, in the city or the country, everywhere some flaw—some defect—some trouble is felt, and yet the inhabitant of the far north could not appreciate the favorable points of the native who has the equator for his home. Everywhere the native is attached to his country, even if surrounded with numerous dangers.

"Nature is represented to you often in quite a crude state. Material is often placed in your hands offering no attraction of beauty, but by the accumulated knowledge handed down from generations you are enabled to fashion a thing of beauty out of the rough material, putting it in shape and adapting it to its wants. The higher civilization rises the larger will be the demand of the coming man. Hundreds of things and objects you find necessary to live a cultivated life in a large city are not of the slightest consequence to the savage; he could not derive any benefit to amuse himself out of it, for the thing requires mental and physical training, or it must be learned how to work it.

"Necessity, also, as I previously remarked, plays an important part. Every young bird hatched requires the killing of so many more insects for food; every new baby born means thnt the new creature wants a certain amount of food and room. The farmer in possession of one hundred acres of uncultivated land, may sustain himself and wife upon so many acres of cultivated land, but if he increases his family by the addition of children the acreage of cultivated land must gradually be increased in order to support them. This applies to a county, a State, a republic or empire equally as well.

"Holland is said to have robbed the ocean of much valuable land, which is in a high state of cultivation now, and thousands of human beings are at present found happy in localities where centuries ago the waves and wind ruled alone. It is now beginning to add many thousands of acres more by the draining of a large sea. But it required great energy, much expenditure of money, and yet constant vigilance to prevent the old enemy from taking back, by force, in a short time where it required many, many years to lock and coax him out. To a certain extent it will ever be thus with your Sacramento valley. The fertile valley must be brought to a high state of cultivation, but it must be properly protected also. Many a home must be created out of crude and uninviting land, and yet by proper cultivation it will be made to bloom and bear fruit, and bring plenty to the originator and worker, for the land is rich and the climate propitious.

"But when the land is brought to the highest state of cultivation, be it to bear fruit or grain, when the improvements are made by which a whole family can live happy and in modern style, it yet must be protected, if built in such a manner that water can destroy all the work of years. High water in a valley like the Sacramento valley is bound to show its force. If one year is passed by and no protection made for the next year, all the improvements may go at one sweep, and this applies equally as well to a city or any other improvement exposed to the force of water. Therefore, it behooves your people, occupying the valley, not only to look to the present, but to commence in seating your children or coming generations more secure, and that signifies, place life and property out of danger, which will require expenditure of money and labor for the present. Will you look to it? Is that the standpoint from which you reason? Do you intend to look into the future and commence to lay part of the foundation to secure your children or the coming generations? There is much to be feared that your people live only for the present, and that means to get a big slice from the pie that's being divided now— 'never mind the future, let's make money now.' It is this only which entitles one to respect and honor, and he that possesses it in abundance or has its equivalent, already exercises more force in your republic than many a potentate of Europe, and keeps himself excluded probably far more from the common lot of human beings than many a noted noble of the old world. Also, in their travels or journeys over your extensive country, this acquired wealth enables them to exclude themselves by chartering a whole railroad car or train, in order to come only in contact with their own class. This remark is made in the year eighteen hundred and eighty-two below. Investigate and compare how far it has been carried out fifty years later, if you still exist."

THE NATION'S DEBT AND TAXES.

"We will now speak of matters concerning the nation mostly, and it will be necessary to be brief, as your absence must not be prolonged," said Lucifer.

"To begin with, we will touch the debt of your country, or the United States of America. Our opinion here is, that it is being paid off too rapidly, which is not at all necessary. Coming generations ought to assist, and as the population is continually on the increase, it will be far easier in the future. Only articles of luxury ought to be taxed, and particularly those manufactured articles which cause so much unhappiness, ought to help to pay the principal portion of the debt in the future. If tobacco causes harm, it would be better if less were used; and thus it may be with your alcoholic beverages, excepting pure wine. Beer and wine ought to be taxed more reasonably, for in those beverages lies a safeguard against intemperance of the grosser sort. People will drink, despite all the phantoms and scarecrows of the total abstinence class. If beer and wine were looked upon more as food and drink, the danger would also be less.

"In regard to the debt, the world must acknowledge that there is no nation in existence who is enabled to pay off such enormous amounts every month. But you have such vast resources, some only to be developed when required, which is another reason why the debt should be paid off more in the future, when the country has become richer, or been settled up more permanently.

"Some of the articles in daily use are unjustly taxed, comparatively speaking. I will only introduce one item, and that is matches—'Lucifer matches,' you know. You put a tax on those, and every poor woman in the land must use them at present. You cannot go back to flint and steel, for these matches have become of as much use as a newspaper, and certainly more than a fine chandelier, carriage, large mirror, rocking chair, or a display of jewelry. All the latter articles could be dispensed with, and must of necessity be by many people, and yet no taxation is placed upon them. The matches are far more necessary than some luxurious food. The tax ought to be annulled as soon as possible, for it is an unjust taxation in comparison with other articles."

QUALIFICATIONS OF CITIZENS AND CANDIDATES.

"Education ought to be made compulsory in every State, as a safeguard. Every boy and girl in the land ought to be made to attend school a certain time every year, so, at least, to learn to read and write. You certainly cannot boast that your people rank first in education, when you have over six millions of people in the United States who can neither read nor write, which would make the percentage about twelve or thirteen in one hundred persons. One of these American sovereigns may be proud of his native country, which permits him to place his ballot, or vote, in opposition to an educated person, who knows what he is casting his ballot for, while the ignoramus relies entirely upon hearsay. No man should be permitted to exercise the right of a citizen who has not acquired sufficient education to read and write, and know something of the laws by which your country is ruled. If a foreigner, who cannot read his own language, or does not desire to acquire the English language, he is hardly fit to make a good American citizen. To speak plainer still, it is high time to exercise more judgment in rushing your new-fledged citizens on the stage of action. Be positive first that the man makes a good citizen and is intelligent, for out of this class sometimes your officers are chosen. If candidates are not qualified by education to hold an office, they ought not to be placed on the ticket to be voted for; but even if elected, they should be prevented from taking the position.

"The people want more intelligence from their officers and servants who manage the public affairs. And not only intelligence is required, but honesty is greatly needed for the present and future. No manufacturing company, railroad or steamboat company, or large mercantile firm, chooses men unless they possess some reputation in the branch for which they were chosen; why then should the people of your country have men put in office to manage public affairs and handle the necessary funds, if their knowledge or education doesnot fit them, and are besides dishonest? In large cities of America this is of considerable importance, and much of the mismanagement may be laid at the door of incompetents. But, despite the lack of brains in their head, it is so balanced that 'self preservation is the first law of nature,' so at the end of their term it matters little whether the public suffered or not, they themselves did not, financially. Very often the salary from the office somehow made them rich, and being that, means likewise to be highly honored in your country—in fact, of the two, having the brains in the head in one, and the equivalent of brains in the pocket of the other, the latter is thought the most of by not a few.

THE JURY SYSTEM.

"Some change is required in the jury system. The rule that in a verdict the jury must be unanimous, does not agree with the present age. Out of twelve men, the majority ought to rule, just as in any proceeding of societies, companies, or in your legislative halls, when laws are enacted or important questions are voted upon. Also the idea, because a man read a newspaper report of a crime, he must be incapable of performing jury duty, is quite behind the age, allowing only the more ignorant to act as jurors, for every intelligent citizen reads some local paper every day at present. Many criminals would be more justly punished by an experienced judge than twelve jurymen who never heard or read about the case, or not formed some sort of opinion when they did read it. However, this is a question in which no haste should be exercised, as judges are human too; can rule inhumanly and be corrupted also. In some of the older conntries where they desired this right for a century or more, and have now got it, they have become already tired of it, for it takes up much valuable time of those who are drawn as jurors, and who are mostly engaged in some kind of business. The fact is, nations are pretty much like children. A rattle in the hand of an infant causes a desire of the other infant to possess one also, and when it has one it is soon thrown away. If there were not some wise men at the head of some nations, with flexible and strong nerves as well as back bones, the nation or family would often suffer, as some members would show themselves unruly. There must be a MUST placed before the unruly member of the family, or the rabble of large cities, for if they were permitted to carry on their style, society generally would suffer. Of course the cry is, 'liberty is suppressed,' but the toleration of such liberty means the destruction of a city or the governmsnt of the country in the end, and against this every well meaning man and woman must be opposed.

TOO MUCH LIBERTY TO THE YOUTH.

"Your young people enjoy too much liberty, which often is turned to wanton vandalism, and frequently injury is inflicted on themselves. This applies principally to boys, and young men under twenty years of age, who ape after their elders, and frequently at an early age have acquired habits which physically and mentally would wreck even the older and stronger men. Is it any wonder then that many die before their time? Where lies the fault but in the want of strong nerves and the back bone of the one who represents the house or family? At an earlier age it is the mother who molds the child's mind, but does she do it properly? Something is wrong in the management of the children. No such politeness is shown to the aged and strangers as in other countries. The latter, if but lately arrived from another country, may receive instead of politeness, only mockery, vile epithets, or feel the hardness of a brickbat. This is not overdrawn, as you well know, Mr. Smith, for you are aware there is a certain class of human beings sojourning with you, to do menial labor principally in your State, who frequently have been murdered even by boys. Was there ever one seriously punished for it? If so, how often were the criminals punished, and how severely was such punishment meted out to the culprits?

It is necessary, probably, to inform you that in the station we occupy, we cannot show any favoritism. We cannot in our way of judging the souls of human beings, put you in the front ranks, simply because you represent yourselves as Caucasians and the followers of Christ's teachings, but carry out little of His acts. Would it be just to ignore the disciple of Confucius if he acted more honorably than you, even if you were a reputed follower of Christ's superior teachings, which you never carry out. We judge the acts of men. The white race is not better than the yellow, nor is the yellow better than the black, owing to its color or professed religion. Therefore our opinion in the ill treatment of these so-call yellow heathens, differs somewhat with you, although we attach no blame to you in endeavoring to preserve your nationality, or take as immigrants those who are more related to you as being of one type, similar religion and civilization. But when you permit your youngsters or brutal men to carry out criminal acts, often unpunished, your boasted Christianity is open to some doubt. This is no attack upon the teacher, but upon the pretended followers.

"Boys in every country will show their spirit—the young animal does, also—and the parents of both animal and man are obliged, in their peculiar way, to caution, guide, and protect them until strong enough themselves. If a boy shows animal spirit he is by no means wicked, even if he has his little fun here and there at the expense of others, elders overlook it; but just as soon as wanton destruction of property takes place in a city, when the monuments of the dead are mutilated, houses burned down, the weaker sex publicly insulted on the streets, men knocked down, and a supposed inferior race illtreated wherever brought in contact with them, then fun and sport has ceased—the boundary line was overstepped and judicious punishment must be served out; and if the head of the house has lost control of such children, the local or State government must take charge of them. Far better and more profitable to the State than under safe iron doors and strong locks years after. Of course, you catch the hares before you cook them. The boys have to be caught also first.

DEMORALIZING LITERATURE.

"The literature, too, that the young of both sexes have access to, and visible all about your cities, has a bad effect when read by them. Upon the imaginative young man or girl, the pictures and stories drawn and reported have often a more serious effect than gross reality. At the last the yet pure mind would be disgusted, while in the pictures art displayed itself, being inviting and overdoing itself generally. The sophistry adopted in some of these stories is so subtle that the youth can hardly suspect that any wrong is meant by it. Thus murder may be covered up by the gallantry displayed in behalf of a young woman, and the murderer put forward as the hero, although he may subsequently ruin the girl and make her the vilest of the vile himself; his crime in the end consists only of a trifle too much of youthful folly. The young people whose minds devour and store up such bad readings may, in course of time, think themselves justified in carrying out acts of which they have read so frequently as being only youthful indiscretions. Such reading is a subtle poison to the mind, which, if persisted in, will gradually but surely show its effect sooner or later.

"Reading at the present wields a powerful influence, and will in future be increased. What was formerly communicated to you in words the newspapers and telegraph can put in your mind in shorter time. The editor or writer is therefore not only representing his profession alone, but he can act the minister of the gospel and school-master or the moralist and teacher also, and if the last two are wolves in sheep's disguise the morality of the people must be debased and brought lower as the power of the press increases of that class.

"Many of the pictures and descriptions of your flashy newspapers are unreliable and untruthful. It is true, the work is well finished and the artist has learned, by drawing on imagination, to embellish his pictures to please his patrons. They draw quite well—deeper and deeper, nearer and nearer, many a youth in the same direction, and place them right upon the same track to be propelled backward to the dumping off place of filth and misery.

"Of course the public must have its wants, either naturally or artificially, gratified. The restaurateur prepares his food as demanded, the manager of a theater must procure plays that 'take,' and probably the publisher of such journals, laying bare and illustrating the vices and wrong doings of a nation, dishes up his mental food to gratify the lover of arts and the student of the higher literature. (?) If the government of a country can tolerate this sort of liberty to its young people, the mother may just as well allow little Johnny to devour all the jam, preserves, and sweetmeats together and expect the boy will grow healthier, wiser, and improve generally.

"Do you not think, Mr. Smith," Lucifer continued, "that the sophistry of some papers, in combination with some noted politicians, had something to do in the execution of a recent great crime against the very head, or chief of your nation? The mind of a man that is weakly balanced, and has had access to such sort of reasoning, may think himself justified in having carried out an act by which the whole world was shocked, and one need not be surprised if a man of such a diseased mind does think himself a benefactor to mankind, and a martyr too. In order to hem in, or curb this increasing mischief, you must have just and influential men appointed in every State, or large city, to act as censors of the press and its illustrations. You prohibit obscene pictures to be exhibited, and make it a criminal offense. Often such pictures are as pure as is the mind of a child to that of a debauched person, when compared with some illustrations in your papers. A picture of a human being, or a statue, may be represented perfectly nude, and yet remain pure; or, in other words, awaken no impure thoughts, while the half-clad representation of a human being may suggest a corrupt thought to the mind of a half-grown youth, or an intelligent child. In this much, over-much hypocrisy is exhibited, which you seldom meet in the older countries. Pure statuary and paintings, representing nature truthfully, even half-clad, or unclad, has not a tendency to lower the standard of morality in a nation, while the unnatural position, the connection with the surroundings, or even the disconnection, may have a tendency to make such an exhibition immoral. To the pure, most things appear pure; to the 'I want to appear pure,' very many things would be open to criticism, for such a person would like to make a display of an article he or she does in reality not possess, otherwise than as a counterfeit.

"On the same principle the young people are frequently judged. A certain class would rather have their young act like old men and women, than to make any display of youthfulness. What is this but hypocrisy? A young man or woman, with no spirit or animation, no liveliness, is one in whom nature has taken very little interest, or who has been stricken by some disease, or great sorrow, but the latter will, in course of time, be overcome even. Often such a being may be less pure in thought, but has learned to control his actions, so frequently judgment can be mistaken. The young must have recreation; they cannot be cooped up in your day, night, and Sunday schools, or churches, all the time. If the mind is to be developed healthily, the physical part of the human being cannot be neglected.

RATIONAL RECREATION FOR THE YOUNG PEOPLE.

"The narrow-minded views of some classes of religionists cannot be placed at the head as a guide. Such people see sins sticking out in every direction. The devil is let loose, in his various disguises, to lure the young to him. Thus almost all the pleasures of youth have a devil behind them to destroy the one who indulges in them. The devil who causes the greatest mischief is, according to our way of seeing things on your world, intemperance. You do not learn when you have enough of the pleasure. In your country, many things are overdone. Even over-study, over-work, and too much praying, might be termed intemperance.

"Rational exercise, dancing, riding on horseback, swimming, athletic games, fencing, boxing, archery, shooting with pistol and rifle, and similar in and out of door amusements, can be indulged in, and in the exercise of some the young man or woman need not be debased. Some of these exercises may be extremely beneficial, not only to the person practicing, but also to others. A person who can swim well, may thus have acquired a more useful knowledge than that of dancing, and a person who has learned to defend himself by natural means, may not resort to arms, and thereby kill his antagonist.

"Walking in the United States has found but little favor thus far, excepting in drilling the soldier. It is often wiser to walk than to ride in your fine vehicles, which may give you pure air but not the exercise necessary, which the body requires. It is true there have been numerous walking matches quite frequently indulged in by delicate women, in which the mind, or superior will power, forced the body to unnatural performance for the sake of gain, and was from beginning to end an unnatural transaction. No such intemperate exercise or torture to a human being should be tolerated any more than prize fighting or carrying out duels. There is nothing in such undertakings that has a tendency to elevate mankind, and this may be applied when an animal is used to show its superiority over another.

"A man goading two animals to mortal combat, so that one is killed, the other maimed for life, cannot be a moral benefactor to his race. There are too many in your country who would be only too glad if the animal was sacrificed upon which they staked their dollars, provided the horse came out victorious. Such undertakings have no connection with rational exercises of the young and old, and ought to be put down as cruelty to animal and man. Bull fights and cock fights take off the finer feelings of man. No such idea in the carrying out of bodily exercise is meant. Moderation and temperance in all things.

HIGH PRETENSIONS IN MORALITY TESTED.

"I have long ere this been convinced that angels cannot be made from the average boy or girl, man or woman, before their time. The matter has been explained to you that none are perfect who arrive from below, or not one in ten millions who can be placed in a certain grade, excepting from the lowest round of the ladder to the higher elevations. Any nation which pretends to possess more morality, which pays more attention to religious matters, which boasts to have the most churches, which generally puts itself forward in everything good and superior to this life and the hoped one beyond, believe only when you have examined how many go to their schools and colleges, and how many they keep confined in their penitentiaries and insane asylums. Read the papers and mark down the crimes committed every day. And at the same time closely observe how the laws are executed, or whether the rich are served the same as the poor; whether the man who steals thousands is served the same as the one compelled by want to steal food to save his family. Have your eyes about you for one week, part of night included, to witness for yourself how temperate and pure the people are. Then only, and only then, form an opinion and give in a report. That is the way we do at our periodical visits below. We investigate like your true scientists before we believe and make out our report, We find only too often criminality running riot amongst the very class who pretend so much.

ARBITRATION IN PRIVATE LIFE.

"Frequently much money and property is lost, lives sacrificed and made unhappy, and many things occur which only required a few kind words and all would have been well. Instead of that mankind resorts to law, demanding its right (?), or to brute force and the deadly weapons, and the least (sometimes the hardest of all), is when they use words. The consequences are a lawsuit and so much expense, or the financial ruin of one or both; a murder or maiming for life, and the serving of so many years in the penitentiary. The separation of two young people who love each other, but who have not learned to control their hot tempers; the words applied in passion went deep into the hearts of both parties—the language used was never meant, but one thinking itself injured had to resort to the same weapon, applying stinging words; a divorce is applied for, and in the meantime, the passion having cooled down, love returns, but pride prevents supposed humiliation if one or the other acknowledges herself or himself the aggressor, and the law takes its course, causing a separation of two human beings, and probably children too—only a few kind words not spoken in time.

"I only give a few instances, but it will be sufficient to gain some idea what can be done without resorting to any of the above systems. You have wise men sitting at your Courts as judges, who interpret the laws and adjudge the criminality or injury done. To these men salaries are paid and they are supposed to be honorable men, but why should there not be a set of honorable and just men who precede them, who adjudge or give opinions equivalent to law, without a necessity to commence a suit? I refer now, if you do not fully comprehend the function of the office, to ARBITRATION. Two or three honorable men, and in some cases women, could settle many a lawsuit and family quarrel, and in many cases bring to a head at once difficulties which generally end only in blood.

"It is strange that nations termed civilized have not yet learned the benefit that may arise by appointing or electing men to such offices. Even between nations, many difficulties could be settled (and have already been settled). If unattended to, the nations drift into war, then destruction to life and property, and a general disturbance and misery, continuing for years. Between the employer and employe this method would also be of the greatest benefit, but this matter has already been touched.

REWARD TO WIFE WHIPPERS.

"While matrimonial matters have been mentioned, it may not be out of place to give our opinion regarding those gallant and brave men (?) who periodically beat, kick, and generally ill-treat their wives in the most wanton manner. Such a high stage of civilization (?) should be rewarded with a suitable recognition befitting the case, and as the applicant gradually advances in the art, the honors should accordingly be increased. Say, for instance, the first case be rewarded by placing the applicant for the high honors upon one of those small, long-eared, docile-looking animals, known as a borro or Arizona donkey. Let him be mounted tailward, with large labels back and front, informing the world that this is one of the champion wife-whippers. A drum and fife might enliven the scene—spectators could be gathered as the march is made through the town, and at intervals the numerous 'small boys' might be placed, whose duty it would be to put sweet fragrances over the body of the honored, by throwing some very ancient eggs at him, as suitable ointment. The second honor should be pillory at the public market place or any suitable site. The third honor, give him so many lashes on the bare back, and if his wife has still sufficient love for such a man left, it would probably be best to let him exercise himself, if they are bound to live together as man and wife, for one has to go to the wall before long. I am quite aware," said Lucifer, "that this sort of punishment does not agree with your present stage of civilization, but on the other hand neither does the treatment the man inflicts upon his wife. If ordinary punishment does not reach the conscience of such a man, extraordinary methods must be adopted, just as in violent diseases, it requires unusually strong medicine—kill or cure, you know.

"We, who put the sexes more on equality, judge them accordingly; with you the toleration is rather one-sided. What would in a young man be termed wildness, almost amounts to criminality in a young woman. If woman is dishonored by committing an act society forbids or frowns upon, why should not man? If it is criminal or a dishonor, it must be equally so for man or woman. But your customs have it somewhat different; the least incautious act, often only the animation of youthfulness, dishonors the young woman for life, and none are more severe than her own sex with her. A young man in the gutter may redeem his character in a short time, even if he has moved in the best of society, but let his wife or sister forget themselves, or by some means be found in the same condition, and probably that woman is ruined for life. There is no redemption possible, for she is shunned as the impurest and vilest thing.

"There are many of the so-called demi-monde who would be compelled to lead a different life were they not sustained by men, and frequently the best of men in society, 'the would-be good men,' who would be shocked in public by being addressed by that class, find their India-rubber conscience but little stretched when they are at home with them. Those men, sometimes with wife and family, excel the young men in their devotion to these women. Some excuse might be offered for the young man; first his youthfulness, and secondly married life, particularly in your large cities, has become a very expensive affair, and the expectations of your young women, or young ladies as you denominate them, are very great. The Grand Wedding and AUXILIARIES alone may have a tendency to frighten any ordinary young man whose reliance to sustain two in style depends entirely upon his brain or muscles.

GRAND WEDDINGS.

"These weddings, in order to be fashionable, have to be carried out on a grand scale, going often far beyond the means of the contracting parties, in imitation of some young people who were really possessed of the wealth they chose to exhibit at their matrimonial alliance.

"The majority of these grand matrimonial 'splurges,' where the young people had not sufficient of worldly goods to keep along on the track they placed their matrimonial car, end in never being heard of again excepting at a court of divorce some years after. The young man who allows himself to be made one of the high contracting parties of an expensive or fashionable wedding, making believe that he is enabled, without injuring himself financially, to live in style as the beginning has shown, is either a very weak minded individual or an impostor, and in either case one or both of the parties must suffer, it being only a question of time, sometimes a very short time only.

"Would it not be more rational to enter matrimonial life less ambitious, with less of the grand PRELIMINARIES, but as you advance and have learned to live well together, have learned to pull right ahead in your matrimonial yoke, then have your periodical meetings or anniversaries, and then and there have a happy time of it with your children and friends. This would be commencing small and ending big—the other commences big and ends in nothing, or in a divorce. Some of your most successful men in business and the professions have thus commenced. They began at the lowest round of the ladder and ascended. The custom in most cases is to reverse the order, that is, commence above and walk crab-fashion. Let candidates to these honors reflect upon this question; it is worthy of notice, and the money expended for the useless exhibition would often be better spent if applied to the wants of the future family.

GRAND FUNERALS.

"Not only are your weddings too imposing and costly, but the ending of life—the funerals—are too often carried beyond the means of the family. There is a reform needed in that direction, for it is not necessary to imitate the rich any more than in a wedding. If a rich family sees fit to make a great display of rosewood coffins with gilt handles and all the usual things custom demands in high life, they have a perfect right, if they do not impoverish themselves. It may even be beneficial, for thereby so and so many of the poorer class have needed funds put in their purse for services rendered, or in other words, money distributed amongst the needy. In order to follow those higher in social life, it happens too often, however, that the family must be robbed or deprived of money necessary to their existence. The monuments erected at your burial places are put up on the same principle. If the wealthy family has its thousands to spend to erect a costly monument above or near the grave of a member of the family, they will distribute some money they do not need and in the hands of the poorer class is of some benefit. The money expended for such a purpose could be better applied to those who are living, if they spend beyond their means, or the family is not able to do so without depriving itself. If such money be applied, for instance, for educational purposes of the children, it may do more good than erecting monuments for the dead with inscriptions frequently the opposite of the living. It matters little to the body in either case; both are demanded back to Nature, and destruction and decomposition must take place, and the more rapidly it is carried out in close proximity' to large cities the better it will be for the health of that city.

"With us here, Mr. Smith, it matters little what has been done with the cast-off garments of your souls; you may place tombstones and monuments at their graves, informing the world, or the present and future, of the many virtues they possessed while in life. Here the real virtues are found, and the more numerous vices, sins, or crimes, or whatever you may be pleased to term them, also. It often happens that the deeds of good men are not recognized until centuries elapse. Many of these men and women had barely a mark placed at their heads, and their places of rest are unknown, but their good deeds live, their works of art, the creation of the soul, their poetry, their works of fiction, their music, sculpture, and discoveries in science live, and will live as long as your little world exists. They have no use to place a sign there, signifying that the body of a good man has crumbled into dust; but there have been cases where the people erected monuments, or recognized the virtues of a criminal, made criminal because the man had courage to sacrifice his life against an injustice, or where might ruled and had to be obeyed, whether the individual considered it wrong or not. Such a case happened lately in one of the cities of Italy, where a monument was erected in behalf of one burned four hundred years previously. It took the world just four hundred years to recognize a man's good deeds, and what does his soul care for it now? We knew him at once when he came; we treated him as he had lived; the grand funeral, the burning at the stake or on the pile, does not alter the case with us. All must be prepared and propelled forward, and to accomplish that is the prime duty intrusted to us.

ADULTERATED FOOD AND QUACK MEDICINE.

"Some investigation is necessary by the Government, or the government of every State, of articles of food sold often under high-sounding names. The vessels into which your preserved meats, fruits and vegetables are kept, should also be examined; likewise the numerous compounds, or nostrums sold, causing such miraculous cures and incalculable benefits to suffering humanity, as the advertisements inform one. (?)

"Some of these nostrums may be harmless to health; nevertheless, they are a fraud, and others may be, by the large quantity consumed, actually dangerous. Some of these wonderful (?) drugs are given out as a benefit to mankind, and are manufactured by strict temperance men and pious religionists, but as it is desirable to reap the almighty dollars, it is necessary to make the great remedies palatable, and for this purpose poor alcohol and glucose is just as serviceable as a good quality of alcohol and sugar. It also represents a larger profit, a thing your would-be benefactor of mankind never loses sight of in all his benevolent work of that class. The consciences, you see, of such individuals, are somewhat elastic—often very much so—and, of course, under the guise of medicine, good and spurious alcohol loses its power, and the unfortunate addicted to its use would not recognize it under the very wholesome disguise in which it is introduced, consequently no after-craving for it is expected. (?)

"Millions and millions of dollars have been and are being extracted from the public annually, and by an inviting advertisement almost any liquid and solid can be sold in large cities, and at a profit which will make the manufacturer wealthy, if the public approve the remedy.

"A great deal has been said and written about stock gambling and similar inducements to draw the much-coveted dollars from the dear people's pockets, but it is a well known fact that there are individuals in your country who have made large fortunes in manufacturing articles said to be of medicinal value, and yet possessing no such virtue, or very little, if full credit is given. It might be said that the people control their own purses, and that they are gifted with reasoning powers, nevertheless, it must be admitted, there are many who have faith in these pretended nostrums, and spend their money in the hope of effecting a cure. One affected with a certain disease, either imaginery or real, after reading a puffed-up advertisement, which appears to have been written precisely to fit his case, would blame himself for not having done his duty if he had not, at least, tried one bottle of this celebrated remedy, which an angel handed down (on the label) to the great benefactor of mankind. If the State or General Government does not intend to stop this somewhere, the nation will have to suffer in the end.

"This kind of honesty is already undermining the character and integrity of your nation abroad. When a certain class of merchants send cotton and wool to Europe, loaded down with sand and stones, some one will be compelled to sustain the loss, and in the end it will be the whole nation. The grain, too, is frequently not much better treated, and many manufactured goods, preserved meats and fruit, are put up in such a manner that the purchasers must sustain losses. There is a certain kind of preserved fruit which may be looked upon with suspicion. Such fruit as contains a large quantity of citric acid will attack the tin cans if the sheet tin is not pure, and the solder drops into the fruit very often, and as the same contains a large proportion of lead, the solder is dissolved, and lead poisoning will be the result.

TESTS FOR LEAD.

"Some of your newspaper men rail against tin, but it is not much to be feared if pure; the trouble is with that which is associated with lead. Are these men aware that lead is cheaper than tin, and that nearly all the ordinary tinning is mixed with lead at present? It is the lead to which attention must be called. The tin foil now used for many purposes of manufacture is sometimes half lead. It is true, the lead is packed inside, but in the rolling out, here and there cracks occur, and the lead is exposed, and when brought into contact with certain bodies, it will be attacked or dissolved, and if this should be associated with food, lead poisoning may occur.

"One of the tests of the foil being pure tin is by taking concentrated acetic acid, and a drop let fall upon it will dissolve the lead, producing acetate of lead; if, then, another drop of a solution of iodide of potash is added, a yellow spot is the result, being iodide of lead. By using a drop of bichromate of potash, it also causes the same shade of color, which is, however, the well known color known as chrome yellow.

"Another test is, to moisten the leaf, or foil, with sulphuric acid, which produces no coloration if pure tin, while, in the presence of lead, there is formed a black spot.

"A person who has acquired the knowledge to use the little and very handy instrument known as a blow-pipe, can acquaint himself, in a few seconds, by means of the oxidizing flame and a piece of charcoal, whether lead is present or not, and the tin can, at the same time, be distinguished from lead.

BAKING POWDER.

A great rivalry takes place in your newspapers, where long-drawn advertisements appear, praising up a certain article of manufacture—a chemical mixture might be more appropriate than manufacture—as there is no such thing done. Well, each producer puts his article forward as the simon pure material, the only medium that will raise your biscuits, cakes and bread (and sometimes stomachs too), by means of carbonic acid gas evolved. All the material passed out by competitors are branded fraudulent and dangerous to health, his being the only genuine and CHEMICALLY PURE compounds. This benefactor of families sells his chemically pure (?) compounds as cheap as the others (who make, of course, a similar claim), and throws in a chromo, or a French clock, or resurrector of the dead, in the bargain. Now those who know the compounds used in this mixture of the so-called 'baking or raising powder,' know that every salt almost, used in its composition, costs more if chemically pure than he or they sell a pound. Where is the profit then? But even if these compounds should be chemically pure, some would, if used to excess, cause eventually trouble. There is no doubt some of your people have had their health affected by the constant use of these compounds. These powders are by no means as harmless as the public looks upon them. While there may not be death, there may yet be considerable indigestion stored up in the constant and excessive use of these dough-raisers.

"Not long since one of the leading scientific papers of your country reported carbonate of ammonia used for raising cakes, or the same purpose as the baking powders are used, generally perfectly harmless. This may be true only, providing the ammonia is all expelled as well as the carbonic acid. The latter, although death to any warm blooded animal when inhaled, in a pure state, has no particular effect in such small quantities in the stomach. If, however, ammonia is still present in the food, your scientific gentleman who wrote the article would find, if he partook of the cakes, that quite a commotion would be caused in his bowels, and he would wish that ammonia was doing mischief somewhere else. If you have no faith in my words, only try the experiment when you return. It will not kill the first time, but let me assure you, the test on yourself is not over pleasant.

"Then there are other articles in use every day which are nearly in all cases adulterated, and even to such an extent that the adulterated article in use is itself again adulterated before it is mixed with the genuine article. Generally the material used is harmless, but not unfrequently substances are used by the ignorant which may be absolutely dangerous and extremely obnoxious, as in one of the cases in London, England, where the dry and decomposed wood of coffins, of the color of chiccory, was ground up to adulterate that article, which then, as a mixture, was sold to the manufacturer of coffee. The addition to the coffee must have been as fat and palateable as the reported good ale from the brew where the fat brewer fell into the vessel and his fragrant extract was incorporated into the much loved beverage of Old England.

"In the adulteration of the spices, the adulterants are in most cases not of much better material, and for the examination of that even, a glass of water and a magnifying glass can give you two separate proofs, while a common microscope will further substantiate the truth as to its purity.

LADIES' BEATIFIERS.

"In this may be included the high sounding and pleasing names used as auxiliaries in beautifying your ladies. Also those compounds said to effect such wonderful cures in restoring nature's deficiencies, and many hair dyes are absolutely poisonous, and while one person may escape the effect, the other will have to suffer from it. Silver and lead salts mostly are used, and the latter metal, when used even as a comb, has caused poisoning of lead, just the same as bismuth white will sometimes cause serious poisoning when the face is powdered with it, by some lady. If the powder is pure no danger may be feared immediately, but nearly all commercial bismuth, from which this white face powder is mostly prepared, contains arsenic, and this is the substance to be feared, when the pores absorb the poison. The bismuth salts prescribed for medical purposes are also very often impure, containing arsenic, and of which fact the druggist, and even the physician, may be unaware.

"Right here I must say a few words against the use of these beautifiers when used as such by your females. To consult you, Mr. Smith, you certainly do not, nor any man of common intelligence, hold a young woman in higher estimation because she smears and bedaubs herself with paint and cosmetics, paying attention to hair, cheeks, lips, and eyebrows, to enhance her beauty, or as she thinks, to appear naturally beautiful before you or her admirers. In most cases the art is overdone, and so clumsily carried out that a man would have to be a born idiot or less not to be enabled to look through the disguise. The females in your country, on an average, surpass their sisters in Europe in beauty of the countenance if not form, and many have not the slightest reason to paint 'fraud' upon their faces, for they are handomer without it. Yet, when you look about all over the land, in your large and smaller cities, you may witness this unnatural display—even from girls thirteen or fourteen years of age. Nature generally does not display her work thus. The women with natural red cheeks are robust and strong limbed, not delicate and pale creatures shut up in houses. And yet a delicate and natural looking young woman may possess as much if not superior beauty when compared with those who are favored with a red color in their face. Those who have practiced this habit from their youth up, will find that they require larger and larger quantities to cover Nature's deficiencies. If you cover the pores of the face with powder, it will not stop the natural evaporation known as perspiration, but it may have a tendency to enlarge the pores, making the face then appear very coarse, when not properly tricked out to 'cobweb' the eyes of men. It is similar to arsenic or opium eating, alcohol or any stimulant producing unnatural excitement; the quantities must be increased in the future to be effective, and then it has become an absolute necessity most difficult to eliminate.

"Let your yonng women consider before they resort to the means mentioned, and further let them be opposed to being squeezed into one of those model-form-molds which the inquisition of Spain might have adopted as a torturing machine or instrument.

MEDICINE ADULTERATION.

"Returning to the subject of adulteration, I will add that it may not be generally known that even your medicine is adulterated, and frequently your druggist, calling himself a 'pharmaceutical chemist,' may not be aware of it, mainly because the title without the requisite knowledgs gives him no real advantage, although it may throw sand into the eyes of the public. That in such cases great danger must arise to patients must be obvious, for many drugs used in medicine are poisonous, therefore given in small doses. If then the physician uses his formulas they will be ineffective. The quantity of the drug not being sufficient, a larger quantity must be administered to be effective. Admit now that in another case the same medical man prescribes the same quantity of poison to be put up at the same drug store, but the party takes the prescription to another store which may be nearer or be preferred, and there the poison to be used is pure and fully effective; what will be the result in such a case when double the quantity is used : In one case it is · ineffective and may cause death, in the other the quantity does its work more effectively as it kills at once, if not the proper remedies or antidotes are at hand ; and for all this the physician may be able and qualified for his position.

"The fine, brilliant dyes now used for fabrics, cause poisoning and eruptions of the skin, because the aniline colors nearly all contain arsenic, which is also absorbed by the pores in some cases, while the body is in a state of perspiration. The effect is, however, not positive in all persons who wear much material.

ARSENIC TO FATTEN CATTLE.

"In the use of arsenic direct, there may be mentioned the very latest from Europe. The white arsenic is now used for the fattening of cattle. It has long been known to dealers in horseflesh that for a time arsenic, in certain quantities, mixed with food, or tied in a little bag in such a manner that it is dissolved by the saliva of the horse, and thus very gradually absorbed, has a tendency to improve the horse's appearance, giving the creature a fine, glossy coat. It is necessary, in order to be more effective, to increase the quantity, and as in the case of all similar drugs, such as alcohol, opium, chloral, hasheesh, etc., it wants more and more, and if stopped, then the trouble arrives. As man is served, so will be the animal. To some extent arsenic is used by your women who are constantly before the public, and ever desire to appear youthful. The drug will claim its reward sooner or later, I assure you.

"Able chemists of Germany and Austria have very lately ascertained that if arsenic is fed to a cow the poison is fully absorbed into all its tissues in eight hours. In the milk of such cows the poison was found after five days in one case, and twenty-one days in another. Goats and sheep experimented upon with the same substance were killed. The larger intestines, scrupulously washed and cleaned, and pieces fed to dogs, caused vomiting and diarrhea. To the fowls of the barn-yard, fifteen to thirty grains of blood from the last mentioned animals caused their death. Experiments on smaller animals showed, as in horses, when applied in small quantities, that the animals (cats, rabbits, etc.,) were improved; in larger quantities the heart was affected in its pulsation. The peculiar effect arsenic acid (white arsenic) has upon the system of animals is the difference in the change of food (described as stoffwechsel) in the evacuation, which amounts from twenty to forty per cent. less than in ordinary fed animals. It seems from this, that a saving of the material of the body takes place, which is added to it. Further tests of the meat of such animals proved that neither by long boiling, frying, or baking, is the poison extracted or drawn out from such meat. In European countries, of late, the flesh of horses is sold, similar to the meat of cattle. The danger is obvious if a horse should be used for such a purpose. In the case of the cattle fed with arsenic, even if beneficial to the stock raiser, it would require the greatest carefulness, for such cattle should not be slaughtered for a number of days, and if not fed with the drug, will become lean again.

FRAUD REJUVENATORS.

"Then the highly praised liquids, oils, and pomades, that will cause hair to grow on the heel of your boot, if only enough of the 'magic' is used, are, in some samples, highly dangerous; in others, perfectly harmless. Oil, alcohol, water, glycerine, some fatty matter and essential oils, constitute the whole secret of the great electrical wonder (?) when an analysis is made. This is supposed to have the magical effect, providing faith is strong. The main effect is, money finds its way from the pocket of one person to that of another, and that is about all the change that takes place. The gambler often returns more.

"Many of these nostrums, reported by advertisements to cause such miraculous cures, when all the science of noted physicians is exhausted, ought to be analyzed; even when patented, they should, when suspicion arises, be looked into. When anything of known danger is placed before the public, the sale of such articles ought to be prohibited by law, just the same as flour would be when mixed with an adulterant substance known to be dangerous to health. There are many articles for which civilized life has found daily use, which require investigation also.

IMPURE ICE.

"In your large cities of the United States a very large quantity of ice is used, and in most cases the ice itself is introduced into the liquids and beverages to be consumed. Do you know that much of this ice is not pure? Do you further know that pure ice can only be frozen out of pure and wholesome water? If the ice is not frozen from pure water, the water from the ice under a powerful microscope may open your eyes to what you drink on your very hot days without previous investigation. Your great temperance man (?) is invariably an ice consumer, and such a person may look with horror upon the Teutonic beverage known as 'lager beer' or 'lager bier,' but in nearly all cases the beer is the purest, for the water has previously been heated to 100″ C., or 212″ Fah., and thereby all organic matter destroyed or caused to drop to the bottom of the vessel. Pure air, the light of the sun, and fresh, pure water, play very important parts in the health of a human being, and in large cities every effort possible ought to be made by the authorities (of a city), to secure at least what is possible to furnish. Give sufficient air spaces, as in parks, and here and there place fountains to cool the air and supply the thirsty with pure water. Great attention ought to be paid to cleanliness by ice men, and no stagnant water should be used intended for ice which is likely to be introduced into the liquid to be drank.

"It is well known at present that organic matter is not entirely destroyed by freezing, therefore contagious diseases may be propagated and introduced to a whole town, by using such ice. It is ignorance and the love of gain that causes such troubles very often, but the governments must look to these shortcomings, and at once condemn the lot, by preventing its sale. There must be men appointed whose duty it is to investigate all such matters, and when such men are appointed, political trickery ought not to be brought into play. Such offices are not the kind to reward some ward politician, who has helped to hoist some favored candidate into a prominent and lucrative office, and the latter now endeavors to reciprocate for the service rendered, by placing the other wise, good man into an office in which, owing to the deficiency in his education, he must perforce play the ignoramus, or leave the charge to a deputy, which is only too frequently the case in your country. According to our reasoning here, the chief of any department, be he of the kitchen or where it requires the highest attainments for the supervision of his office, ought to be in all cases fully qualified for his position.

"A number of instances might be mentioned how food can be adulterated without causing any injury to health, the object being simply to compete with the trade and make a big profit, but it is hardly wise to remind your trades people, or tempt them to distinguish themselves (?) more than they have already.

WATER ADDED TO LARD.

"I will mention one case, for instance. A certain butcher produces beautiful white lard and gives full weight, and this fine article or brand he is enabled to sell at a less rate than his opponent across the street, whose product has a yellow tinge and seldom full weight. Why is this? Oh, because the first butcher knows how to mix water with it, and his neighbor has not learned the trick yet. Don't blame the first one too much, nor bestow an unusual amount of praise upon the other, for the man across the street would be just as ready to mix water with it if he knew how the thing would mix."

"But water and fatty matter does not usually mix."

"Oh, quite well, Mr. Smith, if you know how. A child could carry out the simple combination, and there is not the least harm, excepting water being cheaper, for which one pays instead of fat. In subjecting the fatty substance to a gradual heat, the water is expelled or evaporated, and thereby the quantity can be ascertained, but the substance mixed with the water is more difficult to ascertain. Only a chemist can probably ascertain that. But you take that every day in your food, although associated with another element or elements.

"These are profitable but harmless adulterants, but ignorance has caused, many times, very serious troubles. For instance butter, in order to give it the fine, yellow color, so much liked, has chrome yellow incorporated. The color is a compound of lead, chromium and oxygen. The two metals are both poisonous. This color is also too often used by confectioners, and when a large quantity of yellow colored candy is consumed, may cause serious trouble without guessing the real cause of the disturbance in the child's health. If yellow color must be used, annetto in one case, and saffron in the other, both vegetable yellow, are recommended. The most wholesome is that in which no color is used at all.

"I will shorten the subject but add that your country is still a novice in the art of adulteration. It is often so clumsily carried out that a person even with limited knowledge can ascertain or acquaint himself of the genuineness of an article by simple tests and experiments. In the older countries it is often necessary to call in experts to know whether one has a genuine article before him or an imitation only. But as previously remarked, all bodies have some characteristics which they will exhibit under certain conditions, then showing their qualities. Say, for instance, you mix lard and butter, color it to suit the taste, in order to make it look inviting to the purchasers, of which you are one. The taste is deficient, and a doubt as to its good and genuine quality is raised. Simply put the substance in a test tube, place in boiling water, and when melted let it cool gradually in the water, and when cool it will be found that the liquids as they solidified arranged themselves according to their specific gravity, and then the salt, sand, or heavy solid matter is at the bottom, next will be butter and the upper layer lard. Within a few months they have used the oil of cocoanut to adulterate butter—the same test can be applied. The adulterant is not dangerous, but the butter becomes rancid rapidly.

COFFEE ADULTERANTS.

"The same principle may be applied to your coffee. If doubted, drop half a teaspoonful into a glass of clear water; if coffee, it will float for some time, but chiccory, being differently constituted, will fill its cells and sink to the bottom and in a short time discolor the water also, which coffee does not for some time. Moreover, chiccory contains starch, and may by the use of a solution of iodine show she characteristic blue coloration of starch when brought in contact with that chemical reagent. Then the microscope will show different formations, even if you mix and grind in one mill, for all bodies divided into small particles will still exhibit their characteristic body under the microscope, although the eye cannot perceive the difference. It is far more difficult in coffee or tea to discover a fraudulent article, when the genuine article (like tea or coffee) has been mixed with exhausted or used material of the same sort. Then only the strength of a genuine article will be a guide to its proper value, and by comparing the diffusion of both the quality is exhibited. Quite a number of instances could I give upon this subject, but your time is limited, Mr. Smith. We must pass over to something else of note

SEWAGE.

"The disposal of the sewage in your large cities is also of very great importance, and it requires not a great deal of scientific knowledge or foresight to predict that in some localities serious troubles will arise, and that the methods you have adopted will in the end prove themselves very costly and dangerous experiments. All those who have any knowledge of a gas, know that it is a very difficult matter to keep it properly confined without leakage. If then you build big cisterns in loose soil and these devices placed close to your houses, and from them run into it all your refuse matter, gases must be generated when shut off from the atmosphere. If the plumber has loved you well, charged you well, and done his work well, the gas may not find its way direct to the house by the devices adopted. But it will in the course of time; but the worst comes when the soil itself is perfectly saturated, like an old grave yard, and cannot hold more.

"In large cities this question is of no small importance to the health of its inhabitants; therefore in the supervision of the laws enacted, regulating and enforcing sanitary matters, only men of knowledge and experience should be appointed to office. The time is not so distant when the refuse matter and rejections not used in the building up and reconstruction of the human being, will prove itself of immense value when given back to the plants from whence it originally came, or has been taken as food by animal and man. At present millions are expended in money for fertilizers brought from distant islands, where it has been stored up for ages by the feathered tribe and marine animals. The first named rejections, after necessary preparation, will prove itself equal, if not superior, to the best imported guano, used mostly in Europe at present.

LABORING CLASS SAFE INVESTMENT.

"I have still a word to say in behalf of the laboring class, and that is the safe investment of their earnings.

"In a country like the United States of North America, it is expected that the people are sufficiently intelligent to know what to do with their surplus money, and yet there are millions of men and women who cannot, or do not, employ their earned money to advantage. Some have lost faith, for in their efforts to draw large benefits from it, they have sacrificed the whole. It is, therefore, preferred to spend the money earned for enjoyment, rather than lose it, as previously had been done; and this has several drawbacks, and the main one is, a human being grows older, and ought, therefore, lay by a 'penny for old age.' What the working people want is safe Government security, at small interest, but POSITIVELY SAFE, or as safe as in other countries already applied. Your wise law-givers and law-makers ought to give this question early attention and some consideration, as it is of considerable importance.

"I am aware some bill was introduced establishing 'Postal Savings' Banks,' and that might, if carried out, produce some benefit; but other efforts ought to be made in behalf of the working class in this direction, and there is no doubt that methods can be discovered which would meet the case, which is particularly necessary in large cities, for there the facilities are ever offered to spend the money easiest, so easy that one Sunday will swallow the earnings of the six working days.

KEEPING SUNDAY.

"This brings me to a subject I want to express myself upon, and that is the keeping of your Sunday, which, by the more religiously inclined of your nation, is also termed Sabbath, using the Hebrew term, and with it its signification, which, probably, by your early Puritans, was carried out or imitated for the best; but the nation has changed somewhat since, many thinking it no sacrilege at present to bake their pork and beans even on the Sabbath. In the

Western States, where the European is most strongly represented, the idea of spending Sunday, as they call it there, is on more liberal principles, particularly in the larger cities. The day is looked upon not only to have religious principles inculcated by listening to prayers and sermons in churches, and in sending the children to Sunday schools for religious teachings, but it is also thought to be a day of rest from labor, and may, as one chooses, be reserved for rational recreation and amusement, which the working class cannot have during six days of labor.

"The views taken by the so-called religious people are, in most cases, extremely selfish and narrow-minded, and if their ideas could be enforced, it would have a tendency to increase the already large number of religious hypocrites you have in the United States.

"Take, for instance, the thousands of young people employed in factories and shops in New York (or other large cities), six days in the week, beginning and ending at certain hours. As the places where they are employed are in many cases long distances away from where they live, it naturally takes away much time, compelling them to rise earlier in the morning, and shortening the evenings. Then the terrible heat the people have to suffer in New York, in summer, not only in day time but also at night, when it is frequently the most intolerant, has also an effect. Now, when Sunday comes, these people want fresh air and recreation, which, without doubt, from a standpoint of health, is more beneficial to them than to be resting in their close quarters, or listening to long sermons, as man should live to be saved (?). The 'would-be savers' take generally good care to have their rational exercise during the week. The daughters of the man whose whole family belongs to the high-toned church, have their fine vehicles, drawn by superb horses, and driven by a liveried coachman. to ride to the suburbs and parks, where fresh and invigorating air can be inhaled six days in a week, but in the meantime the three or four hundred girls and women in the factories of their father are industriously employed, not only in earning wages, but also employed, by the work they necessarily have to perform, in destroying their health. The daughter of the rich inhales the pure atmosphere, enjoys the light of the sun and the beautiful landscape and surroundings, while the factory girl must inhale the dust-laden air and particles whirled about by the machinery in use, in the manufactory they are engaged in, be it organic or inorganic matter—some of it in either case is often absolutely poisonous when inhaled for weeks, months and years. If, then, the working girl seeks fresh air when Sunday arrives, is she very much worse in morality than the daughter of the employer, or the daughters of the rich who find it to their advantage to attend church Sunday morning, and not always because religious feelings predominated in the matter? A young woman, as well as a young man, may have various reasons and attractions for attending church, which may not have the remotest relationship to any religious feelings a human being may entertain—in fact may be in direct opposition to it even. These matters must be left with the people themselves, for the young girl who thinks it to her interest to attend church will do so. And it may be for her interest, while in another it may be destructive to health and have a tendency to shorten her life.

"As political questions will bring one man to side with one party while his friend or foe may side with the opposite, so in these religious questions will there be different opinions, but Sunday or Sabbath, call it what you like, MUST FOREVER BE SET APART AS A DAY OF REST, devoted to religious teachings, and all rational and moral amusements. Neither the religious class, nor those who advocate that Sunday should merely be a day of recreation, should override each other. Each class must be protected and check each other when they become oppressive to those of opposite views.

"The law should be such as guarantees to every working man and woman, physically or mentally employed, one day of rest out of seven, and those whose duty compels them to add to the pleasure of making others happy on Sunday, should have an equivalent time granted during the week, to put them on equality. If the barber, livery man, baker, cook, engineer, brakeman, and those of similar occupations, are by their occupations compelled to be on duty on Sunday, another day must be allowed to them, to grant them the requisite enjoyment. While to a certain extent trade and traffic may stop on Sunday, it is impossible in some occupations to carry it out, in all cases. The steamer on the ocean and rivers cannot shut down on its regular work without sustaining great losses, and causing a great deal of dissatisfaction, if not danger. Nor can the keeper of a hotel devote that day to a fast day, and thereby give the cooks and other employes the usual rest.

"Cleanliness, which is said to be next to godliness, cannot be curtailed, and therefore bathing establishments and barber shops ought not to close until at least noon has passed. Some great manufacturing enterprises, as that of iron, glass, porcelain, and similar industries, cannot shut down on Sunday, unless great financial losses are sustained, but in all such cases the working man or woman must be protected by giving them an equivalent in money or rest. By all means give them the time, if you want them to hold out and be serviceable to you.

"Continued work will not cause your people to become morally better, and the holidays you have are too few, or of that nature that the days can be enjoyed for pleasure, amusement, or recreation. All this must, more or less, depend upon the Sunday; but if your laws are so construed or carried out that only one class is protected, it necessarily must be an oppression to one or another faction opposed to each other. Therefore, it is wise not only to keep a Sunday from the religious standpoint, but also for the sake of recreation and innocent amusement.

"The observation made in the large cities of Europe is this; that during church hours, principally in the morning, the streets are kept perfectly quiet; but if the weather is fine in the afternoon, the people cannot be cooped up in the city, but a very large portion finds itself attracted, according to its social standing at different localities, one of the great attractions being the Zoological Gardens, to show the children the animals as nature represents them. Your straight-laced religionist would probably not consider it any sin if his smaller children were engaged in looking over some book where the same animals are illustrated which they may have seen in life at the Zoological Gardens several times during the week. Why, then, should not the less favored in worldly goods be put in a position, with his family, to make himself acquainted with that which is agreeable, pleasing, and elevating?

"If no efforts are made in your great republic by the National, State, or City governments, to create innocent amusement for the working classes, and, to a certain extent, the Sunday, you will find in the end the cost ten-fold. If, by compulsory laws, the Puritan spirit is carried too far; if you curb, sit upon, and smother all feelings to spend the Sunday in a different manner from a class who feel disposed to pass the day in church, you will find that reaction will take place. It will be something like a steam boiler, with a pressure within that the boiler plates cannot withstand. It explodes, dealing death and destruction around it.

"There are people so fanatical and narrow-minded as to show their opposition even to the keeping open of libraries on Sunday, fearing that thereby the people will be gradually drawn away from the church. What is the result if the libraries are closed? Very few will visit the churches, but many may visit places where they can not only read, but find strong drink also.

"In the older countries you may find a large number of very respectable reading rooms arranged upon that principle, where not only the most important journals of the world can be found, as food for the mind, but also more substantial food for the body—liquid and solid, hot and cold. If such institutions were closed, it would not have a tendency to improve mankind morally, for their time would be employed, perhaps, in far less beneficial amusement. Judging from this standpoint, it may be admitted that the employment of a musical corps on behalf of the populace of a large city, may be of no little benefit, if it only serves to draw them away from the grosser amusements to which they are attracted nightly.

"Your politicians on an average are too cowardly, or let me substitute the word 'smart,' to show their cards in favor of one, or the opposite side. They know too well that thereby votes will be lost in such a conflict before an election, but such questions must be settled on a more permanent basis sooner or later. As the United States of North America recognizes no particular religion or creed, as in the older countries, it cannot therefore ignore a very large portion of the people of your republic who profess no particular religion, despite of its being termed a christian country.

"Let all worship the Deity as they choose, they are only responsible for their actions, good or bad. As you have now learned, we make no distinction in regard to professions made. The question is sinply: 'What have you rendered during life to be elevated above another when your soul arrives here?' 'Has your life been so perfect that no faults or sins have been committed?' The power we possess to read the soul makes many a supposed good man or woman only a hypocrite. The work shown below was for selfish ends.

OPINION ABOUT CHRISTIANITY.

"Then you do not hold that Christians are any better than those professing other religions?" I inquired.

"No, if they do not carry out the lessons Christ taught them. It makes a great difference between preaching and teaching Christianity and carrying it out. All nations professing one or the other of the different denominations of the Christian religion, are wanting in the execution of the doctrine taught by Christ.

"The three great religions, not known as heathen, rest principally upon the laws of Moses, or still prior, the laws of the Egyptians, and by these laws the larger part of the world is still governed, or in the same spirit. One day in the week you preach Christianity, and six days the laws of Moses are executed, and very often poorly at that. The supposed good man or Christian is not so full of humility when his right cheek is smitten to present his left for similar treatment; or in other words, if you inflicted insult and injury, like the true nature of the Indian or savage it is his equal desire to return to you coin of the same kind, only in a less savage manner, but probably repaying you in a far more injurious manner than the savage would be enabled to do.

"This is but human nature engrafted into man and the animal, but if you wish to be a real and genuine follower of Christ, then you must have your passions so controlled and subdued as would make an angel of you on your earth below. It is one of the most difficult acts to carry out, to execute the teachings of Jesus Christ, to 'return good for evil.' By all your teachings and professions in the three great religions of Europe and America, it is still eye for eye, tooth for tooth, life for life, and will be, because you are only human beings.

"If the Christians were in a condition to carry out the doctrines of Christ fully, much of our labor would be curtailed, for we would have that class already in a condition to pass over. But your passions remain, causing some good and much evil, and in that, other human beings, professing a different religion from either Hebrew, Christian or Mohammedan, may even surpass you, and in very many instances do, for they are far more temperate in their appetites than the Caucasian race, who mostly profess the first three religions. There would be peace and happiness on earth. Many occupations and tribulations would cease to exist. No war, no quarrels; no law suits, no lawyers for that purpose, no fear of being injured physically or morally by man as our foe. Very many troubles you would be spared, as they could not under the circumstances exist or take place. But the wolf does not lie down with the lamb yet, unless at the very least there is still a strong desire in the rascal to take a good bite from the best portion of the poor lamb's body, and the lion is not going to eat straw like an ox yet, particularly if the quiet and innocent looking ox is to share the same field with him. And man is man still, and he will take advantage of another, be he of the very lowest type of humanity or one of the most advanced nations in civilization, it is the same species still. It is here where the 'finishing touches' have to be applied to the very best of them even, to enable them to make an appearance on a higher stage of progression.

"It is a waste of words and time upon this subject, for from what you have yourself seen and been taught, you must have learned that all the good accomplished must be executed by yourself. What matters it whether your faith is somewhat different from your neighbor. After all the supposed difference, you both believe in the same great Deity. Here, for instance, is the true spirit of Christians as they should act towards each other. A late religious journal mentions the following: 'We have before us the twenty-ninth annual report of the Protestant Kirchliche Hilfsverein of the Canton of Argau, for the year 1881, and one of the most remarkable features in it is the list of kindly and brotherly actions which the Protestant minority has received in many communes from the Catholic majority. At Rheinfelden, the Protestant congregation does not as yet possess a church of its own, although it is collecting funds to build one. Hence it meets at present in a large room; but at the recent installation of a new Protestant Pfarrer (pastor), when this room was found to be too small to accommodate the number of visitors who were expected at the ceremony, the Catholic congregation offered their evangelical fellow citizens the free use of the parish church, which was gladly accepted, and many Catholics attended the service. Such a fact shows a growth of tolerance on both sides.' This," Lucifer added, "is the true Christian spirit and intellectual progress, which, wherever exhibited, will bear good fruit. And here I will add another item, showing the spirit of some noted clergyman who was not full of hypocrisy and deceit:

"'The Bishop of Melbourne, Australia, being requested by a deputation to use prayer in order to produce rain, answered and told them plainly that it would be not only absurd, but useless, to use such a prayer, as the laws of nature and the causes which control the weather are irrevocably fixed and cannot be changed by prayers, which are only intended for spiritual communion with the Deity, and in them only spiritual blessings should be asked. Instead of praying for rain he recommended judicious irrigation to the petitioners.'

"Here, then, Mr. Smith, is no false doctrine and no hypocrisy. Such a man ought to be highly honored for displaying his moral courage. Many a Bishop may hold the same opinion but dare not express his views before his flock. In this case there is great independence and uprightness manifested, not often met with in clergymen. This Bishop, besides, admits that he occasionally smokes a cigar and drinks a glass of wine. Will he be damned for it?

PUBLIC LAND.

"A few words of caution regarding your public land may not be amiss. The opinion prevailing here is that your public land is rushed off too rapidly, cheaply, and in too large quantities, to capitalists of both Europe and America, principally purchased for the purpose of speculation. Look well to your birthright. When a large tract of land is purchased from the government, there ought to be a surety given that colonies be established and the land cultivated, when foreign persons purchase public land. It has been purchased lately of an area sufficiently large to create a fair sized state or kingdom out of it. To a great extent what has been mentioned must apply to the American citizen, when the land purchased is not intended for cultivation. The quantity ought to be limited, at any rate, and a surety given that the land be brought under cultivation, and the smaller the acreage into which it is divided and subdivided, the better the cultivation and yield will be. Let me assure you all the fertile public land you have is needed and will be taken possession of in less than two centuries. Let it not pass into the hands of the rich alone, or else history will repeat itself in America as well as Europe. What that signifies, Mr. Smith, you must be aware.

MORE SECURITY ON WATER AND LAND.

"I will now give you my opinion in regard to protection of the traveling public on water and land. The governments of the civilized world should make trans-Atlantic and other navigation companies FULLY RESPONSIBLE for any deficiency on their steamers, or where not proper safeguards and appliances are supplied in the assistance of saving life by shipwreck or accident on the high sea. It is well known that there are life-saving devices invented of various descriptions, which would greatly aid in diminishing the loss of life by water were they carried or adopted by the ships. The main object is to save money and carry as many passengers and as much freight as possible, in order to produce large profits or dividends to the stockholders of the company. This is, of course, far more agreeable than the purchase of life-rafts and the later style of lifepreservers.

"It is also frequently the case, at these periodical accidents, that neither the crew nor the passengers had been properly instructed in the uses of some devices. The life-saving apparatus ought to be within reach, and the company ought to be compelled to explain to its passengers the use of life-preservers and similar devices. When the accident has taken place it is too late, and the people are too greatly excited to be properly guided and instructed.

"The crew ought to be drilled for accidents generally, including fire and explosions, in order to know how to manage when the danger threatens. If all discipline has ceased on board of a ship, and nothing but fear is visible upon the countenances of the crew, then you may rest assured that a great loss of life will occur, unless a miracle should take place to save them. The greatest attention, also, ought to be paid to the closing of the compartments of the regular passenger steamers. If there were no neglect, many a ship would not have gone to the bottom so rapidly and caused such great loss of life and property. When the ship is caught in a fog, as it is only too often the case in close proximity to England. the greatest attention ought to be paid to preventing a collision. The rate of speed adopted, when thus endangered, is too great geneially.

"A great security lies in the experienced and sober commandant. A man who is addicted to strong drink, that is, found intoxicated, ought to be deprived of his office. The danger is too great even if the subordinate officers are extremely careful, because the commandant is still the ruler of the vessel, even when half drunk.

RAILROADS.

"Regarding the railroads, it may be said that an employe connected with a railroad and holding a responsible position, where it lies in his power through his carelessness or intemperance to cause the loss of life, ought to be made FULLY AMENABLE to the laws of the land, and the companies also made responsible, when proof is offered that a person was employed who was known to be negligent of his duties.

"The employes, such as brakeman and others, ought to have better protection for their lives. There are too many killed and maimed by the old devices that are in use yet in the coupling of cars. Just as it is with the steamers, so with the railroads, the new devices cause an outlay of money by the use of the patented article, and the change of cars, mostly freight cars, for between those generally is your young brakeman jammed into a mass of crushed bones and quivering flesh, to die or to be 'repaired' by surgical aid, which signifies minus certain limbs for life. The law of the State or government should give better protection in these cases, as it is possible to prevent many accidents by adopting improved methods of coupling the cars, or do away almost entirely from that source. The life to the stockholder of these companies may be of little value, but a civilized nation cannot coolly sit by and allow these accidents to be repeated over and over again, when it is known that a preventive is at hand.

"The crossings of railroads ought to be far better guarded than they usually are in the United States. Wherever there are crossings, and where many vehicles have to pass, there guards ought to be stationed, who would prevent careless drivers from endangering their own or other people's lives. Often, too, no danger is feared; for how do they know precisely when a train is due, or passes that particular spot? If the man must wait, he may arrive at his destination somewhat later, but it is far better to obey rules and regulations, than to be cut up in the style your fiery horses have a way of doing. The tracks, when they approach a large city, or even small ones, should be well guarded by high fences, and no one permitted to use them as a sort of highway, or as a promenading place for the blind, deaf, and the nurses of children. Allow no one upon the track but those assigned to duty there. In the United States the greatest carelessness is thus displayed, not only by the employes, but by the people themselves, and in many cases where the companies were financially bled for some gross carelessness, they were not in the least responsible for the life, nor the lost limb of the careless sufferer.

"This may be applied to the loss of animals, also, in not a few cases. It is necessary to look at both sides of a question to be just, as many accidents were and are atoned for financially by railroad companies, where the parties have no claim whatever. The companies themselves must be empowered with certain rights on their roads, at certain localities, and then enforce their rights.

"If a vicious boy jumps on to a moving train at a certain locality in a city, and is run over, how is the company liable for such behavior? It is true, the company is empowered to prevent the attempt, but the officers in charge are not sufficiently numerous to watch at all points, when the roads are so open as they mostly are in the United States, and where every vicious and ill-trained boy cannot be watched.

GOVERNMENT RAILROADS AND TELEGRAPHS.

In regard to railroads and telegraphs, your government ought to begin to make an attempt at controlling some of the main lines. As in postal affairs, since postage has been lowered, the revenue has increased, so would travel increase if the rates were lowered so as simply to cover expenses and a small profit. That very large profits are the result in the working of some roads is plain enough. Men do not become rich and acquire millions unless there is some revenue or bonanza from which the supply is drawn. It is of course not generally admitted. This is, however, a political question, in which very many people are interested, and even if the attempt is made, it will meet with strong opposition, because politicians on both sides are more or less affected by such a change; therefore, for this and other reasons, no change may be expected for years to come. The government, in both methods of conveyance or in the use of railroad and telegraph, ought to be more independent. It ought to control its own lines from New York to San Francisco; then designing men would be curbed in their selfish speculations.

SAFE BUILDING.

"Closer attention ought to be paid to the safety of buildings where a large number of people congregate. Such buildings ought never to be overcrowded, and it is not sufficient to observe these rules only right after some great accident has happened, but to make the rules permanent. The doors of all public buildings ought, of course, to open outward, and safety established against the usual accidents caused by the negligence of man.

"Works where dangerous explosives are manufactured ought to be isolated as much as possible, and not permitted in close proximity to a growing village or town. It is well known that some towns in your country grow very rapidly; if, then, explosions occur, the loss of life and property must be greater—or that sooner or later, an explosion takes place, is an established fact, as the past may inform you.

SANITARY MATTERS.

"The sanitary question in your large cities, as well as smaller ones, requires the closest attention on behalf of the inhabitants. The most able men who have studied the subject should take the duty in charge, and recommend remedies, and when recommended, the town authorities should possess the energy and will to have them executed. No figure-head, or incompetent person, or persons, must hold such a responsible position, for this is not an office specially created for some 'worker' in an election, for whom the chosen candidate seeks employment at the expense of the public. Men who have made special studies of questions in which man is threatened to sustain great injury, be it direct or indirect, cannot be replaced when they hold a responsible office by men 'who are willing to learn.' Should such a person be tolerated who acquires similar offices, any more than a perfect greenhorn who is willing to learn to drive a locomotive, or take charge of an ocean steamer as chief engineer, without having acquired the requisite knowledge and manipulations of the machinery.

MOB LAW.

"About 'mob law' I will say, that better attention should be paid to the security of prisoners who are charged with heinous crimes. The city and county governments, and the State itself, must give sufficient security in leaving the prisoners unmolested, and assuring them of having fair and righteous trials. It has been frequently proved that circumstantial evidence can be such, through various causes, that life may, by hasty executions, like hanging by a mob, be taken innocently. But even if death be deserved you must, as a leading civilized nation, allow the strong (but often too slow) arm of the law to take its usual course. It must be admitted that in many cases the crimes are of such magnitude that only a speedy and also a violent death can atone for it, but haste may cause great regret if the wrong person is sacrificed. No such criminal transaction can elevate a nation. Law and order everywhere over the land must be obeyed, and the criminal must have guaranteed a just and fair trial. In not a few of these hasty and violent executions has it been proved that men engaged in such acts had been previously (and were subsequently) connected with crimes themselves, which would have brought them very near to the gallows, and such men thirst for blood and life.

SENTIMENTALITY.

"On the other hand, there is a sentimental, half-religious class amongst you, mostly congregated in the larger cities, and composed of young, sentimental women, with some older would-be philanthropists, who ought not to be encouraged too much in the methods they adopt in behalf of the welfare of the criminals mentioned. It may be an act of charity to supply a hardened criminal, as a murderer, with clean clothing, and otherwise make him appear as a human being should seem, but when attempts are made to make heroes out of such fiendish criminals who commit horrible and atrocious deeds in cold blood, and without the least human feelings, it must not only lower the standard of intelligence of a people, but it gives direct encouragement to such fiends—puts, in fact, a sort of reward upon heinous deeds. There are deeds committed which can only be atoned by death, and when the proof is clear, no trifling flaw of the law ought to be the cause of retarding an execution. Away with him or her. Hang, shoot, or decapitate them, or use methods that are still more rapid to deprive of life without the slightest noise or unsightliness. Give their bodies to the surgeons to aid science at some medical college, and what is left, cremate, and give the ashes to relatives, if a demand is made, and if not, place the remnant at properly assigned places. Such should be the penalty after sentence is passed, and the more rapid the human being is deprived of life, the more humane it will be, and the less painful. To torture your criminals by the bungling of inexperienced persons in hanging, is cruelty. The law simply demands the life of the criminal and no more. Torture is not meant, but frequently torture is applied. There has been a great deal of sentimentality exhibited about executions, but wherever capital punishment has been abolished, there the crimes increased, because your brutalized criminal only fears punishment when life is taken, or wherever pain is inflicted upon him.

"A late writer, traveler, and statesman, on the other side of the Atlantic ocean, says: 'It is only by corporal punishment, liberally administered, that the horrible brutality of modern roughs, both young and old, can be checked.' Need I tell you, as both countries are similar, it might with profit be applied to your country, and often when incarceration would not have the slightest effect upon a hardened criminal, a little instrument known in physics and to a certain extent by your physicians, would have a better effect, if judiciously applied, than the 'cat-o'-nine-tails.' If the fellow would not tremble at the sight of the instrument the second time applied, he would be courageous indeed.

"Sometimes a good thrashing, applied in proper time to your regular ruffian and bully, has already a very wholesome effect. The dear boy was spared at home when he was young, so the public has to measure out his quota, adding interest too for extra crookedness. But in not a few cases the brute in human shape is imprisoned, overwhelmed with religious tracts and flowers, and a sort of hero is made of him. Those who ought really to create sympathy are in the meantime neglected, as their crimes have not sufficiently matured or developed yet to be thought important enough to tame down. (?)

"This is a sickly sort of humanity, coming from still more sickly religious views. If those people really meant to show charity, benevolence, or their christian spirit, material can generally be found very near, in large cities, far more worthy than the class mentioned, This sort of charity must have a pernicious effect upon the rising generation, for there are thousands of young men who are pushed forward by their vanity and their training to gain prominence, and if their minds are badly balanced, they may even be gratified to outshine others in criminality. To no man or woman of honor and good sense, would a man appear otherwise than a great criminal who had shot and killed another (who befriended him) in the back, and thereby gained some filthy lucre and some sort of reputation or fame, owing to the murdered man being an outlaw. Such men sooner or later will also have to die unnatural deaths. The deed committed is but murder, although sanctioned indirectly by higher authorities. This is using weapons in civil life similar to forbidden warfare by civilized nations. Only your appointed officer can take life, and only when forced to defend himself in behalf of his own life or in the prevention of escape of a great criminal.

"Yet this class of men at your theaters, if placed on exhibition, or take a part themselves in an act specially written for them, draw often full houses, and sometimes one of those idiotic and sentimental human plants of the opposite sex may have a false cupid to delude her heart and head to such a degree that nothing but matrimony will be an antidote to the malady. Generally the time is brief to impress upon such a class of females what sort of a human elephant they have drawn in their matrimonial lottery. Ill-treatment and death has frequently been the reward of such rashness. A wolf cannot be turned into a lamb, nor can it be expected that such men make good and humane husbands, although there may be a few exceptions.

AMERICAN ABROAD.

"Now a word about the foreign born citizen visiting his native country, and there creating disturbances and getting arrested. He demands that the Government of the United States give him protection and cause his release, because it gave him citizenship and made him one of the 'sovereigns' (?) of your great republic. Have you ever reflected, Mr. Smith, about this? It may be patriotic to assist in the release of your relatives and friends when oppressed in a foreign country. Such an act may be overlooked, even if you were a foreigner, which you really are, in the land you visit. As an American citizen, you have no right to visit any European country of which you happen to be a native, and while there, try to stir up a rebellion, or speak disrespectfully of the government where you sojourn. You are subject to the laws of the land you revisit, and while you can rail and find fault against the government in your own country, the same right cannot be expected to be tolerated by the foreign government whose country you visit. There is too much sympathy thrown away in such cases, and a person who has thus got himself into trouble, lacks either good sense, or entertains some rascality which requires a little cooping up.

"If the English, French and German Governments allow its citizens (not emigrants) to visit this country, and while here, they commit acts which the law of the land does not tolerate, what objections could those governments raise if these men were arrested and properly punished? Why should your people expect different treatment? In monarchies, as well as republics, the laws of the land must be obeyed, or chaos and disorder would follow. In plain language, let the foreign born citizen visiting his native country, as Germany, England, and Ireland, exercise some control over his tongue, and he will receive better treatment than when he attacks these governments in their own country, and thus beards the lion. And we may add, whenever foul and cowardly means are resorted to to accomplish an end in a cause, no matter how worthy previously, the methods adopted take away a large portion of sympathy, or diminish that cause.

"There are many, very many things to be righted yet in your world, but reason and the advancing spirit of the age must take hold of them, applying force or gentleness, whichever may be thought most prudent, or applicable. If, however, resort is had to assassination, and other cowardly and uncivilized acts, by which the innocent mostly have to suffer, then such a cause must deserve less moral and financial support than may be expected. It may also come to pass, when grosser and more numerous dark deeds are committed by this, to a great extent, race hatred; when the 'lions' and 'bulls' on one side will become so excited that not a little mischief may be expected from them, and many find their way to this part of those who first began this sort of warfare. Without doubt, much innocent blood would thus be sacrificed, and in the end a tried and courageous nation cannot be coerced into terms, or accept unconditionally what is demanded, by trying to frighten it. In the end these crimes will recoil, with terrible force, on the perpetrators and instigators both.

Those who are advocating this sort of warfare may discover, when it is too late, that they are playing with a two-edged sword, cutting both ways, for between the European, American, and transplanted European, the difference is very small. If dynamite, then, has become the terror of Europe, can it not be transplanted to a country called a republic, and there, for every grudge, for every supposed wrong, cause destruction to life and property? Those journalists, therefore, who are otherwise honest and fair when it concerns the country in which they reside, should not encourage such principles in other countries. If this explosive theory takes possession of the lower classes in large cities, then you may look for a general uproar, not only in the civilized countries of Europe, but, also, in the various countries of America. It will be difficult to say when and where it will end, if the press of any country countenances such criminalities, or tries to find excuses in behalf of the justice or righteousness of such deeds.

PUBLIC SCHOOLS.

"About the public schools of your country it may be remarked, that while I entertain the greatest respect and admiration for learned and accomplished human beings, I find the average man or woman (below) does not require it, and in not a few instances, it may cause injury, if only a smattering of learning is acquired. A solid English education, befitting your country, is far better than acquiring bad French and German. As a traveler, I entertain the highest regard for the linguist, but he must not be deficient in other requisite knowledge.

"At the present age, the better informed class of all civilized nations must pay attention in acquiring the leading modern languages, and after they have mastered one, they will find it of advantage to pay attention to another—just the same as in scientific studies, there are connecting links, and a knowledge of one assists in acquiring the other.

"English, French, and German ought to be acquired, and in your State the Spanish language, and even the Chinese may prove to be remunerative from a commercial standpoint. If any of these languages, however, have to be acquired at the expense of the English language, it will be far better to leave the studies out, or only to those who are designed by their social standing to acquire more extensive knowledge, or to those whose intellectual development is greater.

"Music, being a similar acquirement, could be omitted or taught at home, if desired; but drawing, again, a most useful knowledge in after life, in almost any trade or occupation of both sexes, should not be neglected. It trains the eye for many purposes, and in the use of the finer work of woman is a constant guide, as well as the trades that the young men are to follow in the future.

WANTED.

"The schools generally ought to be better supplied with simple apparatus to convey ideas to the mind of the child. It is far more effective than the language in the books, even when illustrated. Everything should be as simple as possible to the minor classes, and no attempt made to make it appear scientific. The child ought to be made earlier acquainted with some of Nature's laws and particularly our surroundings. At present not even your average citizen or supervisor of a county can inform you what constitutes water, or can tell what gases he breathes. It is true, he is 'posted,' as he calls it, that he breathes air, but that mixture may be variously constituted, according to the locality and circumstances, making an air not at all conducive to health. Simple apparatus or instruments represents the part to be instructed in the best, or conveys the idea to the mind at once.

"Some physiological knowledge ought also to be taught. For instance, why should the child not early acquire some knowledge about the functions of the pores and why you take a cold? The majority, or at least many, of the diseases of the human being have their origin from that source. Can it be too early to acquaint the child of it? There are other matters of similar nature which could be pointed out to the pupils and have good effect when gradually comprehended.

KINDNESS TO ANIMALS.

"Although no direct religious teachings are inculcated in your public schools, it yet would in a moral sense be a great benefit to teach the child kindness to animals. The boy who has learned to stick pins into flies, throw stones at every bird and smaller animal he chances to meet, is very apt, if left to himself, to substitute the Bowie-knife for the pin and a revolver for small stones when he grows up to practice his acquired habit upon his own species. Prevent him by kind words—by force and punishment if necessary. Let him be publicly taught that even an animal has some rights which a civilized human being MUST RESPECT. Torture and the wanton killing of animals, who cause no harm but rather benefit mankind, MUST BE STOPPED. In this, however, it must not be understood that my views are against vivisection when honestly carried out for scientific purposes. To gain knowledge, experiments must be made, and some of those experiments demand the life, and man cannot be sacrificed, therefore advantage is taken of the animal.

EXERCISE.

"Some attention ought to be paid to rational exercise, and wherever it is possible the more advanced pupils ought to receive some instruction in the use of the saw, hammer, plane, chisel, auger, file, etc. It would not only be useful exercise, but also a benefit in after life when grown up.

"After having mastered the rudiments of drawing and acquired the use of various tools, many of these young fellows would have already acquired a sort of apprenticeship, and if subsequently employed in the trades, it would give them great advantage over others. Therefore a half an hour thus spent, developing the muscles, would not only produce wholesome exercise, but it would cause benefits subsequently.

"It is a well known fact, many of your most successful and prominent men were just such, who in early life acquired some mechanical trade. It did not prevent them in after life from attaining higher accomplishments and wealth. A simple carpenter may thus become a noted astronomer.

VENTILATION.

"Ventilation and judicious exercise are two items of a school room to which the teachers must ever pay attention, in behalf of the health of their scholars. A large quantity of carbonic acid present in close or small school rooms, may injure the children's health not a little. In the older countries, the air of school rooms is frequently analyzed, in order to know the percentage of carbonic acid gas (CO^2) present in the room, when occupied for some time, but in your country no attempt has thus far been made, or if an attempt was ever made it was not depending upon instructions from those who rule your schools. The analysis of the gases is a delicate undertaking, requiring care and knowledge in its manipulations, but the quantity of carbonic acid can be ascertained pretty nearly by a very simple apparatus, which every teacher of ordinary intelligence may acquire the knowledge to handle, and he or she be made acquainted with the percentage of this injurious gas present in the room.

DRAINAGE.

"Another important matter is to look to the drainage of superfluous water and refuse to be carried off. If any new devices have been introduced direct into the buildings and school rooms, it should be the duty of those in charge to look well to the safety of the children. The pipes carrying off the waste matter ought to be frequently inspected. Gases, generally arising from closed receptacles where such matter finds its way, have proved far more dangerous to those who are inactive or asleep, than those who are in activity, the latter are seldom injured. This is one of the reasons the plumber himself is not affected, or very seldom. The future generations will and must pay far better attention to these sanitary laws, and they will be more easily executed, for the reason that man has become more enlightened. Ignorance has always been difficult to manage, and truth often gained no foothold, while imposition and charlatanism had no trouble to gain its end.

FOREIGN LANGUAGES.

"It has been observed that where the foreign element is strongly represented, an opinion seems to prevail that their children ought to be educated in the language to which they were natives, or they be taught the mother-tongue of the parents. From a political standpoint, the idea is entirely wrong and defective. The leading language of your Republic is the English, and that language you are compelled to perpetuate, not foreign languages. The law of the land demands American citizens to be educated in the English language, and not to perpetuate a foreign one, be it German, French, Italian, or a dead language, like the Irish. No reasonable man or woman, however, would expect that the parents themselves had no right to have their children acquire their own tongue, which they have learned to speak best.

"The acquisition of languages at the present age is of great benefit, and as traveling to foreign countries constantly increases by better facilities being offered, just so will the demand increase for the requisite knowledge to travel. From an educational point of view, therefore, the encouragement to acquire modern languages must differ from the political point of view. If the scholar's intellect is too dull to acquire even the language of the country, it must be folly to tax the brains of such with foreign languages too. Let such children acquire a common school education and no more.

"No fear, however, may be entertained that any language will supplant the English. All natives, or those who arrive there young, take to the English, and prefer to express their thoughts in that language, and amongst these there may not be a few who disdain to acknowledge any other language, thinking it even a disgrace if one is enabled to express himself in any other language than English. Upon this class my advice shall not be wasted, for ignorance, disguised thus, does not create sympathy in me.

NATURALIZED CITIZENS.

"With this there may be connected another idea prevailing amongst the foreign-born citizens, which ought not to be encouraged. For instance, why should an Irishman or German vote for a candidate of his own nationality in preference to an American or another nationality? And why should an American be opposed to a foreign born citizen, upon the ground alone that he is a foreigner? If all are termed 'American citizens,' it appears that they ought to enjoy their citizenship on more equal ground or terms. Let HONESTY, LOYALTY and QUALIFICATION alone be the virtue and guide by which you elect your officers, and you will be better represented. And this refers to both the great political parties. By all means vote for your American, Irishman, German, or whatever the candidate may be, providing he combines the three qualifications. If one or the other is superior, make the best choice and do not let your little feelings about nationality and religion coerce your better sense to carry out what will always injure the country in the end, and frequently steal money out of your own pocket, if you happen to be a taxpayer. If the man is honorable, he may belong to any foreign nation by birth, and yet be a suitable candidate for one or the other party. There may not be a few localities in the United States where even a negro may be preferred to that of a white man, providing he is elected upon the principle set up as a guide. And why should he not, since you permitted him citizenship?

"There is one class amongst you who, in the larger cities, represent a large amount of taxable property, and yet very few of them, from the various nationalities to which they originally belonged, have held any public offices, thus far, in the United States, and this, it seems, is more attributable to religious grounds than any other. No such narrow-minded views must be entertained in a great republic, whose children must, or should, forever stand on equal ground, as long as the religion is tolerated, or not in conflict with civilization and the laws of the country. As, however, these people represent the foundation of the majority of the American people relating to religion, there cannot be any rational excuse made, unless it is desired to tumble down the old and the new, the Jewish and Christian faith, at once.

I refer now to the Hebrews, who have held back seats, thus far, amongst you, politically, although, as far as qualification and intelligence is concerned, may be preferred to other classes who frequently hold very fat offices in almost every city and town of the United States. A great republic like the United States, which boasts of religious toleration, and offering an asylum to all who feel themselves oppressed, ought to carry out what is said and meant. One thing must be added, and that is, in no case should the belief in a Supreme Being be ignored, for whoever may doubt that, some apparent honesty must be lacking. Remember, there must always be a God, and One who rules over you. If a candidate is deficient in that, he will be deficient in responsibility also, and cannot be trusted to hold a high or low office. The man who acknowledges no hereafter, no soul, nor Deity, should never have the confidence of the people to represent them, or rule over them, although the law of the land may sanction it, or cannot prevent it.

GENERAL INTELLIGENCE.

"As the preceding view upon American citizens and office-holders has some connection with the general intelligence of a nation, a few words regarding it may not be out of place. As far as religion is concerned, it has been observed that the education of the people plays a very important part. It makes the person more tolerant, and his ideas become expanded, or broader views are taken. The educated Hebrew does not underrate the moral standing of a Christian because Jesus Christ is at the head of the Christian religion as its founder. The Catholic does not condemn the Protestant and

Jew because they believe somewhat differently from him, and he has in youth been taught that his church is the only true one, and whose people enter heaven. The Protestant, also, will acknowledge that religion lies principally in carrying out the doctrines, and not in the profession. The views we have here, you have learned and seen applied; they bear a resemblance to your office-holders. All are acceptable if they reach the moral gauge by which we measure your souls.

"The reason the people show their prejudice is because they have not reached a higher standard of intelligence, which mentally empowers them to judge more impartially. From this may be gleaned, that on an average, education is still neglected in the United States, or the whole of the so-called America, and even Europe combined. There is too much superficial knowledge, founded upon hearsay, or what a person acquires by reading newspapers—he has not acquired sufficient knowledge to investigate for himself as to its truth. You may train yourself, or others may assist you in doing it, to sing a song quite well, if you possess a fine voice, without having acquired the knowledge of reading music, or comprehending its notes, but the true art is to study the music and judge for yourself. One offers you self reliance, or to stand alone; but in the other, you must always lean or rely upon some one else who has acquired the learning. This sort of knowledge is wanted more and more in the United States, and all over the so-called civilized world.

"At present, the great lever is the press, or, in other words, the newspapers, and in the number issued every day in your country, no nation can equal you at present. It must be apparent, however, if the reader has not acquired knowledge, receiving his information principally by the aid of newspapers alone, that the information thus acquired must be liable to frequent errors, and not a few deceptions. It behooves your people, therefore, to sustain and encourage the truthful press, and not those who exaggerate and word-paint in false colors for a consideration.

"The press, at the present time, wields a mighty power in the civilized world, and to a very great extent molds the minds of the people, not only politically, but morally, and in every day life. Therefore, a viciously inclined newspaper can cause a great deal of mischief amongst the class who are, by their inferior education and lack of experience, unable to judge for themselves.

SUPERVISION OVER PRINTED MATTER.

"As I have previously remarked, there must be some supervision by the government over printed matter issued in your country, or finding its way there by water or land from foreign countries. If reading matter is thought injurious to the people, and particularly the youths of both sexes, it ought to be condemned as poisonous material to the mind. If a candidate, in one of his political speeches, has lost his senses by anger, or has his brain partially stolen away by King Alcohol, uttering language against his opponent that offends the ears of respectable people, such speeches ought to be prohibited to appear in public print. Such reading has not a tendency to improve the character of one or the other, but it will gravitate towards a lower morality.

"There is too much foul social matter finding its way into public newspapers, gathered up by your 'live reporters,' as you call some of them. These fellows appear to be to the press or work for the press, like the rag-pickers who enter every dirty nook, corner and alley of a large city to find material. The gatherer of rags at least causes some good, for all his material undergoes a purifying process and becomes a product of general use to everybody, while the immoral slum gathered by the 'live reporter' causes only, if read, a contemptible gratification to some people already low enough in the moral standard, and to the better class such reading cannot cause any improvement or elevation. To a certain extent, to this class of cultivators in morality may be added some of the editors of the opposed candidate. About the time one of your candidates runs the gauntlet for an office, the batteries of misrepresentation are touched off against him by the organ of the opposing party or candidate. Is it always truth which the man is charged with? Is there really a human being in your world who is so good and pure in everything, and thought so by everybody, that nothing but praise is bestowed upon him or her? Even if Jesus Christ was to appear once more, he would find enemies and be morally crucified over again in your world.

"If one candidate is elected over the other only because he knew best how to use vituperating language against his opponent, he nor the people have a just cause to be congratulated in electing such a man to any office. Such proceeding will lower the standard of intelligence and morality of any nation. It only gratifies the lower class, and by this by no means the poor or lower in station are meant, but those who entertain such views or are gratified and pleased with the method adopted.

"Both by the press and the parties through their speakers, there should be more tolerance and purity in a political contest. Why should the leaders of a party not take an interest to have its members who carry on the political campaign to use appropriate language, leaving out all vituperations and personal attacks upon the character of the candidate. With the intelligent this political warfare generally has no effect, and as people or the populace, become better educated, it must become entirely useless.

Foreigners sojourning with you, and not sufficiently versed in those political contests, may come to the conclusion, if they happen to read opposing journals, that you attempt to elect criminals for your officers. He may also form the same opinion, if he reads the newspapers in his own country, should he be deficient in knowing the methods you have in the past adopted in such contests.

SUITABLE VOTING STATIONS.

"This, then, is the last item of a public nature before you, and to many persons it may seem unimportant. History, however, will record it differently. When a purer elevation has been reached in political affairs, it will be noted to have been a most crude state under which your nation labored. This, also, you may in the future say regarding the style in which your ballots are deposited, and what makeshifts you have in the places adopted. It is high time that your intelligent females step in and have a word to say in regard to the nation's welfare, and then more taste will be exhibited in choosing places better fitted and furnished for such purposes. The fact, the places where the balloting takes place ought to be more united or central, and fitted up for the occasion. It is certainly of just as much importance to have a fitting place to vote upon matters concerning the nation, as it is to have a hall in which to drill your soldiers, or a meeting place for a society. As a man is impressed in church, or at the meeting of some secret organization, so the voter would be when the surroundings corresponded, making the duty performed more important and impressive. There is room for advancement here in every large and small city of your nation. It has been observed many times in the preceding history of your nation that, when the places designed as voting stations or 'polls' were situated in close proximity where alcoholic beverages were sold that the result in the election frequently came out unexpectedly, quite differently, placing men into office unfit for the position they were to occupy. Therefore, the building assigned for the purpose of voting upon matters of a public nature, should be isolated from such localities. Your citizen must not be only free to vote as he pleases, but he should be a sober man in every respect when he is permitted to exercise his franchise.

"I find it still of sufficient importance to add or bring before you a certain matter often not quite understood, and in connection with it matters regarding the household and the future occupation of woman.

SHALL WOMEN WORK?

Your newspapers report through their foreign correspondents, or well-to-do Americans traveling in the older countries, how hard the female has to work, and that she is compelled to do all kinds of manual labor which YOUR LADIES never perform. Particularly Germany, Austria and Holland receive the great sympathy of these travelers, and their advice is the governments ought to improve their people. Neither an emperor nor a Bismark can make changes when forty-two million of people occupy but two hundred and twelve square miles, exclusive of the lately acquired territory which Germany has taken. Probably if you were to take forty-two millions of your people and set them down into Germany, not a few women would have to be occupied in useful pursuits. Even those women who do hard out-door labor enjoy better health and are happier than many of your factory girls in large cities. The lower class of females will perform certain kinds of labor which in your country is expected from the man alone. Many of these women whom you think oppressed by their husbands because they perform certain kinds of labor which their husband does not, yet carry the treasury of the family. The man knows full well the money is safer with his wife, and she in most cases takes care of it. In your country a woman always depends upon her husband, and sometimes when funds are required some begging is necessary it is said. Now, does not the poorer woman across the water enjoy more independence than yours in one respect?

"Your fine travelers, who put up at first-class hotels, ride in first-class railroad cars, and in every way take good care to 'steer clear' of the lower class, have frequently much to say about the inhuman treatment of women in these countries. In their travel through the country they notice a number of women employed in carrying manure on their backs, by the aid of one of those willow-ware devices. A stout young fellow does the loading, the women the carrying. Fault is found with the stout young man. Who is he but the farmer's son, and who are the women but common day laborers hired for the occasion. When one of your nabobs hires a woman to scrub his floor, it is not expected that he himself will perform the work or assist, because she happens to be of the weaker sex, neither could it be expected that the young fellow do the work of these women who were hired for the occasion, and were neither his mother, sisters or cousins. In most cases such correspondents never come in close contact with the lower class, therefore it is impossible to judge properly. But it must be admitted that women know how to work; all honor to them. If Bismark gets up a little fighting scheme, or finds it necessary to defend the land, and must call in all the available male population, there will be still workers in the field, and they will work for their own good, too. When your country has acquired a population like Germany, France or Holland, then there may arise a greater cry if women are not employed in coarser labor.

"It is at present, 'What shall we do with our girls?' The answer should be, now and in the future, 'make them work,' and don't be particular if it is honest and fair employment. It is far better for a girl and the community, too, if she is brought up to render service instead of being a fine lady and live in idleness. One may become the wife of an honest man, if only a mechanic or laborer, and he may find ways to advance himself to wealth. The wife would be a happy and contented mother, while the other female may have passed her time in houses where work is not honored. Industry and idleness have in both cases received their reward. Take your choice from it.

"Your young women, particularly those brought up in the country (meaning the republic), have a sort of dislike to menial labor, and particularly is it obnoxious when rendered to others or when wages are paid as a domestic. Can any rational reason be given why the intelligent young woman doing your cooking and attending to your household affairs shall occupy a lower standard in society than the shop-girl, the one occupied in copying manuscripts, or similar occupations assigned to women? Many of the very best of wives and mothers are engaged in the same occupation, which forever are necessary to any household. There is far too much fastidiousness displayed by young women which should soon be changed to the advantage of the girls. The educated young woman remains still the same even when turned into a servant girl. There are still young men left who retain sufficient good sense to appreciate certain qualities in young women. They do not think the well born and well educated young woman or young lady, as you term them, dishonored because she entertains a love for the home and knows how to act as a housewife. Imagine, now, such a young man in fair circumstances doing a profitable business and about to take a wife; he is invited to numerous families where there are marriageable daughters, amongst which there is one particular family where he appears to be a general favorite. There are three fine looking and educated young women (ladies) in the family, and their ages are very close together. The tastes of these young ladies differ. The elder one has a literary turn of mind; writes for magazines, talks poetry, loves everything that your grandparents admired, looks with contempt upon the present age, and cares nothing whatever about household affairs. The second loves music, devotes much of her time to it, plays excellently, and is well 'drilled' in the music of the old composers, and frequently she takes great delight in exhibiting her art before the public, that is the higher class, and at parties and meetings at the aristocratic residences. She is greatly admired and understands how to dress for public occasions.

"The young man being well acquainted drops in sometimes unexpectedly, and frequently finds the musical female not so acceptable in dress, in fact it might be termed a little lazy, or slovenly. The elder one, though dressed plain and neat, is never found engaged at anything but books. The youngest one is often invisible, but when found she is always occupied in something useful about the house, or takes the place of her mother, who is somewhat of an invalid. When he is invited to take dinner, she does the honors at the table, or often represents her mother.

"No matter when he calls, when seen she is always neatly dressed for the house, and engaged in some useful occupation, or taking the place of her mother in superintending the household duties. When she is attired for outdoor amusement, she appears as well-dressed as her sisters. She is less brilliant in conversation than her elder sister, and less proficient in the art of music than her second sister, but she has a literary taste as well as a taste for music. But what she most delights in is home life—it is there where she wants to shine.

"Now this young man made all these observations, and he has literary taste and loves music, but he is also somewhat of an epicure and consequently a judge of good dinners, of which he had often enjoyed when placed before him under the superintendence of the youngest daughter. If he now makes his choice, where do you think he expects the greatest happiness? In other words, which of the three sisters would such a man prefer as a wife? If you have not the courage to answer yourself, Mr. Smith, I will answer for you, and it is, 'the youngest one, of course, who knows how to represent the honors of the house and furnish a good dinner, which you yourself know how to appreciate.' This is likewise my choice, although eating and drinking is of no consequence to us, nevertheless I understand human nature well, quite well. Bad dinners have caused many divorces in your world and will in the future also, and as in the future you are compelled to eat and drink as well as your ancestors, it is necessary to keep step with the advancing age, learning the daughters of your land how to cook wholesome food, and looking upon cookery not as a drudgery, but as a science and art, which it is in fact when properly investigated. If the lady of the household does not perform the actual work, she ought to comprehend the science of the kitchen sufficiently not to be at the mercy of ignorant servants, which at present is often the case.

"The higher classes could aid a great deal by setting examples as in the older countries, where queens frequently pride themselves in preparing preserves, and the finer work in cookery. Instructions ought to be given in cookery in every city, and in this the wealthy could again render great assistance, and not only with money, but by taking an interest in such matters publicly. This refers principally to the wives and daughters of the wealthy and well-to-do people. Only make a thing fashionable and it will soon show life, and in setting a fashion it requires some noted personage to take the lead.

"When the time arrives and gas has been sufficiently lowered in price in your large cities, much aid will be rendered when properly applied in the kitchen. It will curtail labor considerably with the further advantage of being much cleaner than when wood or coal is consumed. Gas stoves are simply Bunsen burners or copied after the device discovered by Prof. Bunsen. By the aid of the flame of one of those stoves or burners one is enabled to broil a beefsteak in a brief space of time without any previous preparation, as a strong or weak flame can be applied as desired, and the beefsteak can be prepared most invitingly without burning or smoking the same. In the kitchen also the water-bath ought to be used more, then the fine aroma and taste of the substance under treatment would be retained, owing to the inner vessel never coming to a boil, and thereby having all or most of its fine flavor retained. The finest kind of coffee can thus be prepared as thereby you retain the salt and aroma of the bean also. Here again the advantage shows itself when gas is used, for when the water in the lower vessel has been heated to the boiling point, or 212° F, the gas can be turned down to a very small flame and render as much service as if a large flame were used, providing the heat has been kept at the mentioned degree of heat. The idea which prevails generally by people employed in kitchens, that the substance to be cooked can be hurried up, is erroneous, for water cannot be heated above 212 degrees under ordinary atmospheric pressure. By adding cooking salt, however, the temperture can be raised, also when the vessel is under pressure by the confinement the of steam. Considerable fuel could therefore be saved and the expenses diminished if this were better known by the ordinary cook. This, however, cannot be applied to baking, for then a much greater heat is required, and then it may assist to complete the labor much more rapidly.

"You will perceive now, Mr. Smith, that we have even a slight knowledge of the science of the kitchen, and feel interested therein. If eating is one of the most important aids for man to sustain life why should civilized man not learn to prepare his food as best suits his health and palate?

"Improvement must show itself in every branch in which man is interested, and this is a most important one and will remain so until the end of your world.

"But, sir, it is high time to discontinue our conversation regarding matters of a public nature. A great deal more could be added, much of it of equal importance to what has been suggested, but time with us is of great importance, particularly applicable in your case.

"We must return, instead of advancing some distance further, and towards the third sphere. It is too late, and the matter is urgent that you should return to your body below—there is a limit you must be aware. You are mourned as dead already, but ways will be found to bring you to life, when you have returned to your body below.

PSYCHIC FORCE.

"Only one more information and that you have promised already. I refer to 'Psychic Force.'" "Oh! I see that created some curiosity," Lucifer answered, "but it would be better if the matter was left to rest with me, since it cannot cause any harm, while with you and your species it may produce some injury. Some idiots may look at the force I am to describe in a different light, and it may cause them to be guarded in an insane asylum.

"Psychic Force refers to the spiritual nature of man, or the force of the soul while yet connected with the body, and I will point out several instruments by which you can make tests to gratify your curiosity or love of search in such studies when you are again in proper condition, i. e. the body can hold a sort of communion with you and the soul that is now before me.

"Spiritualists attribute this force entirely to some spirit of a human being, and have various methods to hold such communions, one of which is by means of a small table before which several sit down and place their hands upon it. After a certain amount of time has passed and coaxing been done for some spirit to agitate the table, it begins to move or stand on two legs.

"It has been proved that neither magnetism nor electricity, galvanic or static has the slightest effect for or against it. and you may insulate the table and operators by nonconductors, and the table moves the same if the persons are suitable to each other. The mind or soul must show some similarity, some unity or affirnity, when more than one person sits down to experiment.

"With one of the little instruments to be described, every human being of intelligence can make a test, but it will not move for every body alike, nor immediately, but for those who have caused tables to move it will require but a brief space of time to set it in motion. It is only able to acquaint you positively or negatively—moving three times signifying yes, while once or not all means no.

"It also counts. If the methods have been acquired a great deal may be asked without taking up much time, and the questions can be carried out mentally equally as well as in asking in any language. This applies to the instruments as well as the table.

"The benefit you derive from such a source is no better than you receive from a dream. While in the experiment, under discussion, you are awake, the force yet must be attributed to a similar state of the mind as a dream, in messmerism or experiments closely allied to it. No human being has thus far fathomed this peculiar activity of the soul satisfactorily, not even the highest in authority of the sciences have come near it or gave it justice.

"The most of your philosophers ignore this force entirely, calling it a delusion of the mind, but of this error you may in the future acquaint yourself, for the instrument will move and answer in its way if your mind is suitable, or if you are what spiritualists in their language call a 'medium.'

"The spiritualist takes this force to be emanating from some departed soul, and if you inquire of the force itself the answer will always be such, although your mind or thought is in opposition to it. The answers may come from the soul of an infant, which was unable when in life to express itself in language yet, or it may issue from the spirit of great age when it departed from the world below.

"If you take pains and investigate deeper, you will come to the conclusion that this power, spirit, or the soul (I speak now as if you occupied the body), is not gifted any more than the mind that influences you while in a state of wakefulness. What you know is acquired by the aid of the senses. It cannot tell you positively what hour it is, although the town clock may have its big hands revolving about the dial plates right above your house. It cannot accurately inform you, if you take your watch and place it face downward and inquire the time of the day or night. It will answer, but it is inaccurate or like guess-work. If you make inquiries how many people are next door, it may immediately answer and the answer may be false or entirely incorrect.

"What advantage then can such inquiries add to your knowledge? or what benefit is to be derived by such investigations?

"You may gratify your curiosity and be puzzled, but you will never be able to use it as a guide in your intellectual advancement, for that must ever be dependent as it should be, upon your own energy and brain-force.

"You have learned here that the souls are constantly engaged and exercised. And if they were not they would not feel themselves disposed to answer the silly and selfish questions mostly about dollars and cents, love, matrimony and divorces. Nearly all questions asked are of a selfish nature, in which the spirit cannot itself find any more interest when life has departed.

"Have these spirits ever aided mankind? Some of your spiritualists will answer, they have frequently. They aided in inventing machines, composed poetry wrote speeches, and did many things by using man, as the teacher does when he guides the child in the use of the pen and pencil. The same you might say about dreams—many have become verified, but it would be considered very foolish if any reliance was to be placed in every dream.

"No great discovery will ever be made by the assistance of this force, call you it soul or spirit force. The real work for man to rise upward, and make himself acquainted with natures laws, and master its forces, lies entirely with him. No outside assistance is to be rendered by any supernatural means. Nature has its fixed laws and the Deity designed them. There is no alternative. In no other way will man find his way to advancement, and here too you have witnessed the methods adopted. I caution you, therefore, to place no reliance in this force, for which I will now point out more delicate devices or instruments for experiments, all of which can be worked by one person alone, if that person has the requisite power to cause it to move, which is not possible by every person, and but very few on first trial, unless they are impostors.

PSYCHOGRAPH.

"To make one of those devices is very simple and inexpensive, connected with little or no money outlay, if self made. Procure a small, planed board the size of an ordinary book, and in the center, bore or drill a small cavity to act as a rest. Then prepare an upright about six or seven inches long or high, of a size similar to the smaller end of a broomstick. Break the head off of a small nail and drive nearly all into one end of the stick. File the projecting end round and place in the cavity of the board to fit. Now have ready a somewhat smaller board and screw the same to the other end of the stick. If you set this up it will represent a small table.

"In order that the table will move in every direction, you fasten strong india-rubber bands to the lower part of the upright and the foot or lower board, and the apparatus is ready for operation. This represents, of course, a very crude instrument, but tests can be made with it, but it is not over delicate to be operated upon. When spiral springs are used and better work devoted to it, the device becomes more delicate and better results are obtained.

"Another can be constructed to be very servicable and to be used by two persons if desirable. It is made by taking a clock spring and bending it into the shape of the letter U, and fastening the lower part by means of a screw through a hole of the spring to a small board. With this, if properly made, you can give your spirit answers by telegraph when you connect with the wires of a line.

"All work can be avoided by purchasing a small instrument kept by all stationers and known as a "clip," intended by the aid of a spring to keep papers in proper places. In want of that a patent clothes-pin can be made to be of some service when fastened upon a board. This device is always ready, moves rapidly by the touch of one finger and can be carried in your vest pocket when not mounted. This is far the most delicate ever used for such experiments, readily obtained, costing but a trifle, easily carried, and can be used almost anywhere.

"By the aid of liquids and gases, however, instruments can be constructed, a thousand times more delicate, and if you call in the assistance of electricity you could record the answers in Washington, London, Paris, Berlin, Vienna, St. Petersburg, or any distant station where telegraphic communication is had. The actual benefit deriving from it to man, however, would be nothing but curiosity. These experiments, and how carried out, must at present rest with me.

HARNESS NATURE.

" For your race there is far more important and useful work to carry out, as for instance, the utilization of the sun's rays by concentration creating a heat equaled only by electricity and the burning of the two gases, hydrogen and oxygen, or using the heat in a gentler form to drive your steam engines. Or again utilizing the heat to act upon thermo-electric piles to produce heat, light and force by storage.

"Then draw the electricity from the clouds and the earth, change static electricity into galvanic, storing it up for use as the previous. Bore into the bowels of the earth to procure heat. Learn to harness wave and wind properly to perform part of your labor; in fact, harness and bridle nature wherever she shows her forces, and do it by your intellect alone. Why apply yourself to soul force at all and attempt to fathom the mysteries connected with it? Your surgeons and physiologists have not even learned the function which certain parts of the human or animal anatomy plays while the activity of life remains in it. All these mysteries must be solved, or ought to be before the higher attempt is made to search for the essence of the animal known as the soul.

"That the search in the physical sciences will gradually clear up all mysteries you may rest assured, when the proper time arrives, but the soul of man or the life of the animal will never be completely cleared up in your world. But there is progress—the next stage will show you more, but the grosser material must be kept behind. However, it must be admitted, by the force described, some very curious information may be gained; some right in opposition to the religious views of a human being, or as he has been taught. If, then, this force springs from your own soul you must have opposing forces within you, or there is another invisible power within the human being that exercises great control over man besides the soul.

"This force ignores Jesus Christ as a Deity, but approves of his teachings. It calls no religion bad or good, but believes in the actual work, and in this it coincides with us. It also ignores a hell, as painted and imagined by man, and in this you have had some proof and have it still. The advice it gives you is, in almost all cases, chaste and of a moral character. It cautions you against all wrong and desires you to act righteously. When asked about wordly matters no reliance is to be placed in it, as stated previously. Nothing definite is answered regarding the future. It knows no more than any human being, and yet it answers, being correct or incorrect as it, per chance, may be or coincide. No reliance whatever can be placed upon it; nearly all predictions fail. I have named this little instrument the 'Psychograph,' and, if used, it is hoped the rooms will not have to be enlarged in your insane asylums by overstudy about the working of the new device by which you are enabled to communicate with spirits, as some people will perhaps have it."

THE SOUL DISCOVERED.

"One of your late scientific papers reports the discovery of the soul of man and animal. A German professor places the soul before the world by the peculiar smell animals of every species have with man. If the soul is to be judged by this, it would be somewhat unwholesome to have it condensed. The smell would outsmell the devils which your priests painted in imagination several hundreds of years ago. However, if the theory was correct something of benefit could be squeezed out of it, as I will explain shortly. Prof. N., of ——, Germany, sets out that the smell of the animal is part of its soul; so he places two hares into a suitable cage and gives a dog an opportunity to gratify his desire to sniff and chase the animals for several hours until they are almost exhausted or all but killed. The dog's own life is then immediately taken, the nose and smelling organs separated and placed in a volatile liquid like alcohol or ether. The smell, essence, or the soul, as the professor will have it, is.thereby exhausted and found in the liquid. If, now, a few drops be given to a bull dog, or injected under the skin, the dog will sneak away and act as a coward—has, in fact, turned hare in temperament and disposition. Even the courageous lion was affected and showed cowardism in his behaviour when charged with this new liquid. Now, all honor to the searching professor, but the soul part of the experiment—and the discovery of the same, is just about as far off as it was previously, but the effect the liquid has may contain some trace of truth, for it is well known now, that the effect alcohol has upon man is somewhat different, depending upon the purity of the liquid. Good wine is said to make the indulging person happy, inclined to mirth, music, song and laughter, while the 'lightning whisky,' found in the extremes of civilization of your country, has an effect which can only be gratified by quarrels, fights and murder. Is it any wonder, then, when your savage Indians and half civilized white men commit deeds that shock the world? From this point, then, some faith may be placed; but the soul part you may openly doubt.

RETALIATION ON WIFE WHIPPERS.

"The application, however, of this newly discovered essence would be of no small benefit to some people, for it would have an effect similar to cutting off Sampson's locks, where all of his great strength was hidden. I will explain. Say for instance your neighbor Jones over the way, takes it into his head that it was about time to stay out all night to have a good time, or celebrate one of his periodical sprees, when generally on his return his wife is favored with a beating and any amount of filthy language. A gypsy sorceress, similar to the one lately arrested in Hungaria for helping to put out of the way about three hundred good, but old and useless husbands, finds her way in the neighborhood of your town, and prepares, not poison, but the more modern drug which makes bull-dogs perfectly harmless and takes the courage out of lions. Mrs. Jones hears of the arrival, in fact, with many other wives has been waiting for the benefactress, so she is one of the first to supply herself with half a dozen bottles of the hare essence. Jones' period of jubilation has arrived, and the programme was carried out conscientiously. Indeed, at home he did more than his duty or previously. In fact he eclipsed himself, but his wife takes it meekly and patiently this time, which somewhat astonishes Jones, but brute force is never curbed thus; he thinks his duty must be performed.

"When Jones has his great jollifications he generally rises late, and then likes a good, strong cup of coffee. His wife remembered all this, and in the meantime had made her preparation for the next circus in the house. She had supplied herself with a very flexible riding whip, practicing during the spare time on Jones spare clothes arranged or put together, for she did not desire that her first appearance in the circus ring with the new animal to be turned into a a failure. Then all the doors and windows were secured and breakfast put in order. The coffee was pretty strong that morning and more than an ordinary dose of the new essence made from hares went into it. Jones appeared only lightly dressed, to take his coffee, which he thought splendid that morning and gulped it down. His wife kept her eyes steadily upon him and he did not like that, but she continued to do so which made him very uneasy, and by and by he felt a sort of fear overcoming him which caused him to think he had the ague, or that other desease, you know, when they see snakes and similar animals in imagination. Jones looked up again and thaught his wife looked more savage than he ever saw her before when he thought he was doing his duty. He began to fear her and felt like running away, and he was actually impelled to run, and then the circus performance began. The dogs of war, in the shape of a riding whip, were let loose by his former patient wife and he caught it from every direction. There was no such thing as courage in him to strike back—not even a flea would have been killed by him at that time. He only felt like running, but when he tried the doors of the house they were all securely locked, and when he finally got a window open his courage failed him to jump down two stories on a hard pavement below, so he took his thrashing as it was meted out to him.

"His wife belonging to an orthodox church, always paid her debts, and this being a debt of honor, she concluded not only to pay the capital but add a very fair interest too, so she only stopped the circus performance with Jones when he and she herself were nearly used up, like the poor hares in the cage.

"Jones now entertains great respect for his wife and the periodical sprees have been entirely abandoned, because, you know, the thing is too risky. Thus the discovery could be made very useful, and your gypsy sorceress would be looked upon in the light of a fairy when she makes her annual rounds, instead of being branded a murdering old hag and witch, who rides on broomsticks and old goats.

"This drug might play a more important part still. Admit, for instance, that 'Arabi,' the leader of the Egyptian troops, had been acquainted with this scientific knowledge, all that would have been necessary was to charge the coffee or food of the English barbarians with this new essence, and the whole British army would have turned cowards and, of course, been ignominiously whipped. In this case, however, it might have been necessary that the Egyptians themselves had partaken of the jocky-club essence, made up from a lion, bull-dog and a mule, in order to incorporate sufficient courage and toughness to thrash those overbearing Britishers well.

RETURN AND MUSICAL BIRDS.

Then Lucifer rose up and I reluctantly followed, for what I witnessed and had experienced pleased me so well that I entertained no desire whatever to return to the world below me. I thought by prolonging the time somewhat it may be too late to reoccupy my body, but Lucifer divined my thoughts as readily as if spoken or written in words. He answered: "It is utterly impossible, Mr. Smith. The laws of nature in your world, and the laws here and elsewhere must be obeyed. Half-breeds are not accepted here. You must enter this great reformatory the regular way, via. St. Peter's entrance, and then your account must be passed in before your arrival, or in other words, you must have died in some manner. At present you have only half finished your affairs below, and that will not answer the purpose. You must finish your destiny. You must dance a little longer on the stage of life below, and when the fiddler stops, it is time for you to stop also."

We were about to go when I heard a shrill and sharp sound. When I looked in the direction from whence the sound came, I saw a large bird, with white head and wings, and the balance of the body coal black, hop towards an overhanging limb of the tree under which we sat or stood. Immediately, little birds and big birds of all colors imaginable, appeared and arranged themselves upon two opposite branches, facing each other, As in an organ the pipes run in gradation, or the higher and lower notes, just so were they arranged there, and their color blending was similar to the prismatic colors of the rainbow. It was a most curious and beautiful sight, to see these birds and their solemn looking teacher, who had, besides the description given, light yellow circles about his eyes, making the bird appear as if spectacled. He only wanted a baton to look like some Dirigent or Musical Director. Having no instrument, he used his head and claws. By a nod of his head one row began a song or piece of music, the sound being more like musical instruments than the song of birds. When their part was finished, the next row began, and then followed a sort of chorus, when all sang more animated. The first row appeared as if they questioned, while the second row answered, and both being pleased, a sort of thanksgiving followed.

This music was different from anything ever heard by a human being, and it was most beautiful. No words can describe the music, and only those born and educated for music, and acquainted with the highest parts of the art, could fully appreciate it. I only know that the produced sound was the most pleasing to which my organs of hearing ever listened. Sometimes it appeared to me that the whole address and honor was to Lucifer, for towards him they looked, ignoring me entirely. When they stopped, Lucifer remarked:

"A little attention to you, Mr. Smith. If time would permit I would give you a little history of these musicians, but it must be omitted. But how do you like them?"

"Oh it is beautiful, splendid, magnificent, divine," I remarked with enthusiasm.

"The latter word, divine, is the correct one; it is divine music, but this is far eclipsed in the third sphere, here, and the other side, where we have no control yet. We must go."

As we started, the birds all gave a rousing and short song, which probably was equivalent to one of our hurrahs of a political meeting, or as some European bands call it, a "tusch," i. e., when the big bass drum and biggest bass fiddle, big and little brass instruments, all the fiddles, fifes and clarionettes, with triangles and other instruments, are let loose for a very short time, to do their best, or worst, as the case may be, and in the great tumult, very suddenly cease. Something of that sort, but corresponding with the place, the birds carried out, as an homage to Lucifer entirely, I think now, although at the time my soul appeared to have been vain enough to think a share of the honor was intended for itself.

We passed along rapidly towards the direction from which we came, but the passages were different. He probably took a shorter route, for we soon arrived close to the main office, into which, however, we did not enter, but passed along until we reached the passage through which I had entered. Arriving nearly at the entrance already described, he stopped, saying:

"Mr. Smith, my guidance extends no farther. You must now find your way back yourself and as rapidly as possible, and in that I will give you my aid, or you have gained it by being with me. Your duty to yourself and others is to reoccupy your body in your little world below, and there live quite a number of years yet, experiencing the usual lot of man, some happiness with a large quantity known as trouble. Do the best you can in behalf of others and yourself, and that is all that can be expected. As millions before you, your being (that is soul and body combined) is not constituted to enable the soul to walk through that little door St. Peter so very seldom opens. From this you may judge that we may meet again, and then to see you put through the regular course of progression. First to tumble down the ruling passions or else there would have to be thousands of heavens to please you all, and what would constitute one man's heaven upon your world, would prove only, if tested, to be another one's hell here. Draw, for instance, the comparison from the horse jockey and the distinguished scientist. There must be equalization by tearing down and building up, and so reconstruct a more perfect being, which had many faults previously.

LIFE A PUZZLE—DO RIGHT.

"Life after all for the human being is but a sort of dream—often like a puzzle to some of your kind—and they ask, why they were created are in existence? Happiness with you is often measured by the wealth accumulated, but the wealthy have their glittering sorrows, and if they are dissatisfied and want more millions are they happy? Is not the man who earns his bread by the sweat of his brow, who enjoys fair health, has faith in the Supreme Being, loves and cherishes his true wife and both love their fine and healthy-looking children, far happier than your millionaire who sits in a finely furnished room, surrounded with wealth and all the modern luxuries, but troubled with disease which is sure to kill, and affected with the greater disease, how to acquire another million of dollars?

"One dies comparatively poor, but he reached a high old age and trained his sons to be men, and his daughters to be good wives. The rich man deprived himself of a good share of his life for time with him was simply money. He begrudged nature her rest and its laws were subsequently inflicted. The heirs spread the acquired wealth. Many shared in the spoils; there was no love or honesty amongst them, and envy ruled that the lawyers, rather than the brother or sister, receive the benefit. Now compare their real happiness and the results upon others being their nearest relatives.

"'To be content is rich, and rich enough,' says a great poet. If this refers to wealth it carries a great deal of truth, but if it signifies to be content in all things it would set the world walking like a certain animal which has its eyes forward but goes backward.

"No, you must not rest content in all things or no progression would be possible. But whether you act right or wrong, according to the laws of your world, the real beginning of life commences up here. Beyond, after preparation, is found joy, happiness, peace, glory and celestial love, and to all this you acquire the A B C here, since you will not listen to the teachings of the Great Instructor, or are unable by nature to carry it out yourself thoroughly.

MAN A SLAVE STILL TO HIS PASSIONS.

"Man is man still, his passions have not changed. He is still a slave. Once thousands did the bidding of one man, doing work that your beasts of burden and steam engines carry out now. The pyramyids of Egypt were thus piled up, and other great work done in the past ages. Now man is a slave to money, which is also called wealth, when in abundance and owned by one person.

"There was a time when riches were gained by force of arms, now much is gained by low trickery. One became rich from those who had abundance, the present generation tax those who work, and from these draw their riches by giving out false inducements how to grow rich rapidly themselves.

"It is useless to change the matter, man must run his course. His passions rule him still and will until time has ceased to exist. When all are gathered in, then we may glory also, for our work has been accomplished.

"Once more do the best you can in your own behalf in an honest and upright way, and with all you come in contact. Be a man, play not hypocritically, say yes, or no, at once, and make no promises to any human being unless you know how to be enabled to fulfill them. This often causes great trouble. Pay your debts, give to the needy, but encourage honest labor more than charity. Money often causes harm rather than good when not thus applied. Those who refuse your offered labor are not worth any charity. Let not your conscience bother you there. Be just to all, ignore neither Jew or Christian, black, white, or yellow, for you must come in contact with them again, and here they are on equality with you. In whatever form your prayers are let them be sincere when you address the Deity. Ask not for wealth nor pray that God give you fair weather—it is useless. Pray that he give you strength to act righteously, in fact confine yourself to spiritual affairs in behalf of yourself and family. What man prays for is frequently that by which he would be destroyed. There is a destiny and all must run their course from the shortest lived animalcule to the largest fixed stars or suns in distant space.

RAPID DESCENT.

"Take the same route you came, the progress you make in your descent will be sufficiently rapid to redeem your body. Now farewell, Mr. Smith. 'Auf Wiedersehen,' some nations say, when their people separate, and I am quite positive this will prove true—we will meet again." He then shook hands, and I thanked him sincerely for the attention he paid me, and left, passing along,more rapidly than at my arrival. At the main gate, or grand entrance, I passed in opposite direction to the great stream of departed souls constantly arriving, and as I descended the number became less and less until finally I met no more. I was going downward meteor-like at a frightful velocity—at a rate which a being of flesh and blood could not carry out without being itself destroyed. I came nearer the earth, which, from the distance I started, was entirely invisible, and when first seen appeared only as a very small star. It grew larger and larger rapidily as I drew nearer, and soon after I approached the locality I started from, finally the town I resided appeared, and far above, yet I could see my house and look into one of its rooms, where I was laid out as a corpse, surrounded by men and women, one of whom was my wife.

THE SOUL RETURNS TO THE BODY.

They had taken me from the bed of an other room thinking me dead, and it seemed, were about to prepare me for the grave.

I came nearer and went like a flash of lightning through the house, but unlike lightning, meeting no resistance, passing through everything without the slightest hindrance. I entered the body with the same rapidity and fully took possession of it, and then it seemed I had to rely upon my senses. The entrance to the body was effected by the immediate possession of all its parts, the same as if a vessel was exhausted of its air, and then suddenly opened the air would rush in. I seemed to be passing at once through the millions of pores of the body.

It is difficult to describe; but nothing could have been visible to an ordinarily constituted human being, when I arrived. My hearing was remarkable, and I could feel when they touched me, but as the eyes were closed, I was deprived of sight. Although I could feel the touch, and experienced some pain in the position in which I laid, I yet had not the slightest control over my muscles. The body appeared perfectly rigid; not the slightest motion, or sign of life, could I give. A cloth covered my face, which I felt was frequently raised, and some weeping followed, which, by the sound, I recognized as that of my wife. Presently there was a loud rap, and I heard my wife say, "Come in," and shortly after "come in, gentlemen; I am very glad you have come, Dr. Lee." The latter introduced another medical gentleman to my wife as Dr. Simpson, and then the cloth was raised again, and my wife remarked, "it appears to me there is more moisture in the face than when I last looked, which is but a very short time ago, and there seems to be more color, too; but it may only be my imagination. The warmth of the body, you know, has never entirely ceased, and this kept me from having the last rites performed, although he has been pronounced dead. I fear there is not the slightest hope, but I want to do my duty," and then followed some more sobbing. 'Well, we will try what we can do yet, and you must give us permission to carry out an experiment now frequently applied in such cases. Dr. Rumford has paid a great deal of attention to electricity, and is in possession of a large and powerful induction coil used in his physical experiments. It is not one of those small medical induction coils, which produce, generally, only mild currents, but is a much larger one, intended principally for experiments in natural philosophy. If your husband is dead, there is no hope; but if any life remains, the power of the coil will show it in some manner." When I heard that from Dr. Lee, the greatest fear overcame me, for I had some previous experience, knowing what it was to have such a powerful agent applied to one's body.

INDUCTION COIL—ITS USES.

The door opened again, and Dr. Rumford and several other persons had arrived. "Have you got it doctor," I heard one say, and the reply was, "We have everything necessary here, gentlemen—battery and coil—and I would advise you to have no delay, but commence at once; a few seconds delay, and it may be too late. As you will perceive, gentlemen, I use the bichromate of potash battery, of which the carbons and zincs are so arranged as to let them down in the liquid as far as desired, by which very weak, as well as strong currents, can be given. My advice is to apply the current gradually, for it frequently happens that in such cases the feeling remains, but the subject under experiment has not the slightest control over the body. It is unnecessary to inform you, gentlemen, that thereby great torture would be inflicted if we applied the full current at once. This induction coil is so powerful, that when the elements are down, only one-fourth the current it produces would be unpleasant if subjected to it for some time. Some extraordinary experiments can be carried out with dead bodies when they still retain warmth, and the muscles and nerves have not become too rigid. As it is a painful sensation to receive a heavy shock without warning, provision has been made by insulating one of the wires, which is fastened at the terminal to a glass rod, which, if kept dry, is a non-conductor of electricity, which can be handled with impunity. The method I will adopt is by fastening one terminal or wire connected with the coil to the subject's big toe, foot, or leg, or, better still, insert the pointed terminal under the skin, and to the other wire the glass rod is fastened, and to the latter a wet, soft sponge. By the aid of the rod the sponge can be moved to any desired locality, without any danger to the operator. My idea is to saturate a large piece of flannel in boiling water, folding it up several times, and applying it to the region of the heart, and over this the wet sponge is moved about occasionally. The applications are repeated if necessary. Mrs. Smith, you have boiling water, or nearly so; also, some flannel; please accommodate us at once, for no delay must be shown in this case." So spoke, I think, Dr. Rumford. Then some one wrapped something hard and cold about one of my big toes, and drawed it pretty tight, too, which somewhat pained me, but it was all forgotten when I felt as if being scalded near the region of the heart. They had applied the hot flannel. A man called out, "Gentlemen, are you ready? Please let down the elements one-fourth, Dr. Lee," and instantly I heard the buzzing sound of the machine, and felt the smarting and tingling, stretching and contracting of the flesh, nerves and muscles, extending from the lower extremities to the region of the heart. It seemed as if a gentle and equal heat was distributed all through me, and although it was then not absolutely painful, it could not be termed a very pleasant sensation, in spite of the heat being agreeable, which the mild current produced.

One of the physicians suggested that the sponge be placed upon the spot on the head where the hair had become somewhat thin. Dr. Rumford replied: "With strong currents the experiment may prove dangerous, but as we have but one-fourth of the force applied, we may try;" and he touched the spot, and instantly I felt as if my head had grown as large as a hogshead, and still growing larger and about to explode, and at the same time the idea shot through my head, that if this experiment was continued for any length of time, or the force be used to its fullest extent, that I must be killed by it, without being enabled to give the slightest notice that life remained in the body under treatment. However, the sponge was shortly replaced over the heart, and occasionally moved about.

THE TORTURE.

Another burning sensation, in close proximity to the heart, followed, when new flannel was applied, saturated in hot water, and then Dr. Rumford commanded half down. At this the pain commenced; it felt as if red hot ants by the millions had possession of my body, tearing and pulling with their pincers, pieces of flesh from the exterior and interior.

One of the doctors placed his hand upon my body, and I heard him remark: "There appears to be more heat and moisture present and more color, too." Another one added: "But still no signs of life are visible; we must work more energetically." The continued pain inflicted was terrible, and I was in the greatest fear that one of the physicians would once more become "ambitious," and suggest that another application be made to the head. The only confidence I had was in Dr. Rumford, who knowing the great force of the coil, would probably not assent to the proposition. But if he should be suddenly called away, the other two would assuredly experiment in that way, and thereby end my life. My love for life had then fully returned, and as soon as the soul had once more taken possession of the body, I wanted to live; but by all the will power of the mind, not a muscle, nerve or joint of the grosser material or body would move or was under control. Greater force was applied three-quarters down, and such a pain. The ants appeared at a white heat, rolling, jumping, tearing, fighting and running a muck generally in the quivering flesh. Another uncovering and feeling about. "Warmer still; there is hope, gentlemen," said Dr. Rumford. A woman replied, "Thank God." I knew it was my wife, having recognized her voice. "More hot flannel and some blankets too, Mrs. Smith," and great heavens, the full battery power was applied. I now had a vivid idea how that young Russian student must have suffered when they subjected him to this pain, or torture, in order to force a confession from him, and as to who were his co-criminals when the Czar Alexander was assassinated. It is indescribable what torture they inflicted upon me. I was almost positive it would eventually kill me, if I did not force my muscles into moving. "This is a powerful agent, Dr. Rumford," I heard some one say, "and this induction coil must be a terrible weapon to force confessions from a criminal or human being, or to punish them without killing." The doctor was about to reply, in fact had uttered a few words, when some one gave a terrible yell, which was followed by a jump as if one had jumped from a table, or some elevated place. All laughed and tittered, and Dr. Rumford remarked: "Be careful, Dr. Simpson, the battery is in full force." Dr. Simpson replied in a tone as if his feelings were hurt, "This is no laughing matter; I got the full charge of the coil," and I knew that myself, as just for an instant the pain had ceased, when the current was deflected. Dr. Simpson continued, saying: "You see, gentlemen, my watch chain came in contact with the wire below, and as I moved the blanket, I touched the wire that held the sponge and thus got a full charge for an instant. I feel all right again, but my impression is if there was any life in the subject previously, it has been tortured out of him by our experiment." I heard a sigh. "Without overdrawing, gentlemen," Dr. Simpson continued, "the force we here apply to this corpse, or apparently dead man, is sufficiently powerful to cause the big mammoth, which the Academy of Science in San Francisco acquired from Prof. Ward, to take a walk about the room, should the application be prolonged several hours, and several shocks such as I received, would already have sufficient effect to resuscitate the original mammoth they have in Stuttgart, Germany, and subsequently force it to take a waltz about the circus ring." A suppressed laugh followed this, and I felt being touched here and there, and I also felt that my right eye was partially under my control again. I could just move the eyelid a trifle, and some objects became visible.

BACK TO LIFE.

"See the eye—see the eye move," I heard one of the doctors say, and all at once the spell was broken, and with a horrible yell and a jump from the table or boards on which I was placed, I came down on the floor, trembling like an animal or human being subjected to the greatest imaginable fright. The big toe was bleeding and somewhat injured, for the wire was fastened to it and connection made with the induction coil, which I pulled to the floor in my terrible fright to get away. Dr. Rumford retained his presence of mind, for he ran to the battery and drew the elements from the liquid. The current ceased. The battery was saved, it having considerable wire connected with it, and the coil was not injured in its fall, as it fell on a pair of blankets on the floor. The women appeared to have vanished, but as my sight became more accustomed to the room, I espied two lying in a heap, one being my wife, the other her unmarried sister. They had fainted. Dr. Lee, who, although not frightened, yet appeared very much astonished, soon recovered himself and attended to the ladies, who shortly after showed signs of life. Dr. Simpson appeared badly frightened, which may, to a great extent, have been due to the fact that he himself had suffered from the same source, and Dr. Rumford had his induction coil on his arm, stroking it backward and forward, as one does a pet animal. All this took place and was impressed upon my mind after my recovery, in far less time than it can be described, or verbally given, and when the other ladies who were previously present, began to peep through the partially open door with frightened looks, and Dr. Rumford began to apply endearing names to his dear induction coil and torturing machine, I broke out, in spite of the previous pain inflicted upon me, into uproarious laughter. I could not retain myself. I was per force impelled to give vent to my pent up feelings. I did not forget the seriousness of the occasion, or what I went through in mind since I had retired to bed, but the ludicrous sight I had witnessed, conquered all other feelings at the time.

But all honor to the patient doctors and to science. It is to them that I am indebted for my life. It was true what Lucifer said in my dream, or whatever it was, it appearing to me still as if it had actually occurred, it being, in fact, so vividly impressed upon my mind, if not more so, than anything that ever occurred in my past life. If it was not reality, it was as near as the mind of man, or his soul, can imagine or picture it. He said, "means will be found to bring you to life," and it had to come by the aid of man alone and his discoveries; not by spiritual power, or any other source foreign to this world.

Nature seems to say, help yourself, man, and do it by the knowledge you have acquired and stored up for ages in your books, where all your discoveries are recorded, and applied when wanted. Muscle and brain must ever play the most important part in the progress man will continue to make in this world. No outside assistance will show itself, the Deity having designed that all must be "created" by man himself in this world which he does not furnish himself by nature. And as science progresses, man will be enabled to apply the forces of nature more and more to aid him in his various occupations, researches and amusements, and all this must be acquired through his intellect or brain force.

I submit this work to the public for investigation, and the force mentioned in the preceding pages it is suggested to pay as little attention to as possible. Nothing of note, beneficially, from a material point of view, can be gained by it. Morally, if the force acts alike, some benefit might be gained, providing it acts similarly, but as the power rests, or is supposed to rest, with the individual himself, or herself, who makes the experiment, it must also depend upon the organization, or the moral disposition of the mind, soul, or whatever the essence may be which controls both man and animal.

To those who can investigate without prejudice or impartiality, looking upon it scientifically only, the little instruments are recommended for tests, and if it shows no movement in one person, it must not be thought immovable, or the experiment a fraud. In nearly all that man commences, he has to act a sort of apprenticeship, and those who persevere in the act undertaken, manage, mostly, to acquire the desired knowledge, or learn to manipulate an instrument or machine, and this must be applied to this force also.

THE DEFICIENCIES OF THE WORK.

It has been suggested by a noted journalist that this work ought to be placed before the public in the "best of English"—the fact is admitted, but owing to a deficiency in intellectual training while yet in youth, the subject cannot be related as received, and the assistance to reconstruct sentences to make the subject more readable is declined, as it is looked upon in the same light as "stealing other people's brains," or intellectual capital. The work must, therefore, stand upon its own merit or bottom, like a tub upon the floor.

If criticism is to be indulged in against the expression of language employed, the writer and relator will not hide ostrich-like, but rather invite correction, for thereby we often acquire what we need. Those who correct us, therefore, in a just cause or matter must rather be looked upon as friends—not enemies. An open and straightforward correction is far more acceptable than praise or flattery. The latter can cause incalcuable injury to a vain human being, and if such a person be placed in power the mistakes would exhibit themselves in many ways, by which those in lower ranks would be made to suffer.

Further in regard to this work it would be an act of folly to make an attempt to appear faultless before the grammarian and rhetorician. If deficiencies are met they are admitted for the reason already stated. The fault must be attributed, as in many cases, to the necessity of being employed in a workshop instead of paying attention to the art of expressing oneself in written or verbal language at a time when usually such knowledge is impressed upon the youth's mind. Then the object is not to bring the related matter before college professors as a thesis or dissertation on the knowledge how to express oneself most accurately, but it is placed before the average citizen for mental digestion, or as "substance for thought," and if the writer has been so fortunate to awaken views corresponding with what the person read, he considers himself far more fortunate than having gained a diploma upon rhetoric and grammar, despite of entertaining the highest respect and regard for the acquired knowledge in which, unfortunately, he finds himself deficient.

Since the preceeding has taken place I have followed my usual occupation, enjoying very fair health. In mind I often ask myself, was the vision and supposed instruction a dream, or really an occurrence which spiritually was carried out or took place? But the answer cannot be correctly given, for I am no more able to solve the mystery, or the cause thereof, than the public who may see fit to read the matter which has been published.

We all, however, may be enabled to solve relating mysteries when a dissolution of body and soul has taken place.

Until then and after, adieu,

JONES BROWN SMITH.

Sacramento, California, October 3, 1882.

www.ingramcontent.com/pod-product-compliance
Lightning Source LLC
Chambersburg PA
CBHW022136160426
43197CB00009B/1314